THE SELLING CHECKLIST

A Pocket Companion for Sales Success

Andrew Goldberg

Endorsements

"Andy Goldberg and ActionCOACH have been instrumental in the growth of my business. His energy, passion and dedication help drive people forward to set & achieve their goals."

– Steven Smith, Founder and Owner,

The Lead Generation Company

Andy has brought a wealth of sales knowledge to our company in the years that he's been coaching us, and this book breaks down all the critical elements of any good sales process, putting them into an easy-to-follow and easy-to-understand step-by-step guide." –

Graeme Haddow, Managing Director,

Robert Mackie of Scotland

"A sales book from one of the top Action coaches in the world can only be a good thing. I have used Andrew as a business coach for over 8 years. Thanks to his coaching support for me and my business, <u>every</u> year has been our best year ever, including the pandemic year!

As I was reading this book, I realised it is exactly what the experienced members of my team need to step up to the next level. I then realised it exactly what the new members of my team need to step up to the next level. This book will help beginners get off on the right foot and the 'old dogs learn new trick'.

A bunch of sales techniques that most sales people do not know so do not do. Every one is simple to build into your existing sales system.

Using one (just one!) of these techniques increased our hit rate by 9%.

Support with the best mindset on selling and 18 techniques to help your clients solve their problem, not make them buy, what's not to love!

If you convert less than 70% of your quotes, you need this book.

Order taker, product pusher or problem solver. WOW. I had not thought of my team this way. A copy for each of my team is essential!

This book has opened my mind to the techniques my team need to step up to the next level. I now need to buy this for every one of them.

Unlike so many sales books, the focus of this book isnt about tricking the customer into buying but finding out what the customer really needs and giving it to them. How can sales not increase with that mindset?

The checklist aspect of this book is what makes it so relevant. It is a handbook to keep at your side while getting face to face with clients. I need one for my entire team."

– Adam Davidson, Director, BoConcept Scotland

"A cracking insight into how sales should be done from Andy, who has inspired so many people in his role as an award winning Business Coach. Having been fortunate enough to have had my business transformed by Andy's ideas and inspiration as well as shrewd and clever practise, I would recommend a delve into how it should be done from one of the industry's best practitioners. You won't be disappointed!"

– Colin Thomas, Managing Director, Xtensive Ltd

"Andy Goldberg's actions and results speak for themselves. He is congruent with his teachings and he is a great example of how to learn from your experiences to become a great sales person. I am proud to say Andy is a friend and I love to see him changing the world. *The Selling Checklist* helps you improve your conversion rate by being intentional and focused in leading yourself and your prospective clients. Follow the checklist and achieve the sales success you have been looking for."

– Monte Wyatt, CEO,

AddingZEROS Executive Development

"For more than a decade, ActionCOACH Andy has demonstrated a knack for connecting and commanding respect as a leader in our global coach community. He has risen steadily amongst the ranks of high performing coaches, and I have personally awarded him the highly coveted 'ActionMAN' Award. As a Master Coach and Executive Coach, Andy shares his expertise freely and has an abundance mindset driven by the ActionCOACH culture, that helps his clients reach higher levels of success.

The success of his coaching clients comes from Andy's vast career experience in strategic selling, and this has never been better demonstrated than in his new book, The Selling Checklist. In "The Selling Checklist," Andy breaks down a vast and often complicated subject into an easy-to-follow format, with straightforward concepts and maps out key actions steps that will enable any salesperson – novice and veteran – to achieve greater results.

The Selling Checklist brings an element of accountability to the sales process, focuses salespeople to reflect on every step of their process and refine it along the way. This micro-focus ensures no steps are missed or skipped and that your sales team and process is effective top to bottom.

I encourage you to read the book multiple times, making notes in the margins, testing different strategies, and most importantly, creating your own sales checklist based on the principles in this book."

– Brad Sugars, Founder and CEO of ActionCOACH

Brad's Bio:

Brad Sugars, is internationally known as one of the most influential entrepreneurs. Brad Sugars is a bestselling author, keynote speaker, and the #1 business coach in the world. Over the course of his 30-year career as an entrepreneur, Brad has become the CEO of 9+ companies and is the owner of the multi-million-dollar franchise ActionCOACH®.

"We have been using Andrew Goldberg's services as a Business Coach for several years now. As a primarily service based organisation, our business plateaued because of a lack of Sales.

With Andy's knowledge, tools and skills we implemented a sales check-list strategy which has transformed our Sales approach, and ultimately our business.

The 'Selling Checklist' has real potential to be so impactful and should be mandatory reading for everyone involved in Sales. More importantly, it will help set a concrete foundation for Business Leaders and their organisations."

– Drew Westwood, Managing Director,
Wellwood Communications

"If you're ready to achieve higher levels of sales, then read, absorb and use the strategies in this brilliant book by Andy Goldberg. Andy comes from the heart and truly cares about making a positive difference in the lives of others! Do yourself a favor and read this book! You will be so grateful you did!"

– James Malinchak

Featured on ABCs Hit TV Show, Secret Millionaire Best-Selling Author, 25 Books Delivered 3,000+ Talks & 2,000+ Business Consultations Founder, www.BigMoneySpeaker.com

"Andy notched up his sales expertise the hard – sometimes excruciating – way. On his journey to stellar performance, he developed a set of clear checklists and proven scripts. I use them every day, and thanks to this book, so can you."

– Alan Black, Founder, Blackad

"I have had the pleasure of working with Andy Goldberg for many years and his input has radically improved my business. He is a first class coach and this book is a perfect companion to help you stay on track." – Stephen Cole, Managing Director, Cole AD

"Andy played a major role in our business at a time we were aspiring to reach new goals. His experience, knowledge and enthusiasm inspired our team to reach new levels and his teachings still play a major part in our training and development for all of our employees. This book is a must read, written by someone who has made a real difference to people's lives and successes both personally and professionally."

– Mark McCay, Managing Director, The Kitchen Depot

Published by Chesapeake Consulting Limited

Paperback 978-1-7397198-0-7

Ebook 978-1-7397198-1-4

CONTENTS

Author Preface

My first job in sales just kind of fell into my lap. So did my second one. To be fair, I actually nudged my way into those roles through necessity and a survival instinct. Back in 1995, I worked for a private health insurance company in my hometown of Baltimore, in the US. Believe it or not, I got that job through a temp agency because of my one and only skill at the time: I could type. 120 words per minute, to be precise. I'm typing this very page at that same speed, nearly 30 years on!

I had been working in the hospitality industry – managing hotels and restaurants – for a number of years since leaving university, thinking there was a long-term career opportunity for me there and, at the same time, dreading that prospect. I had to get out, but I had no other skills that seemed to apply to the 'normal' world outside hospitality. For no real reason (other than I had limited options), I interviewed at an office temp company, and the first thing they asked me to do was take a typing test at their computer. As I began typing, the lady who was interviewing me came over to watch, and then proceeded to call some of her colleagues over. They'd never seen anybody type so fast! They couldn't wait to get me placed with one of their clients.

Other than my freakishly fast typing skills, I had a university degree, I carried myself reasonably well (i.e. with confidence) and I had some management and customer service experience. So, when I look back now, I suppose I wasn't completely useless.

They placed me on temporary assignment with a small private healthcare company's sales team. My job was to set up their new CRM system and essentially bring their office into the 21st century with a bit of computer technology and efficiency. The assignment quickly converted from temporary to permanent, and I quickly got to know the salespeople on the team. I watched them with admiration, respect and, to be honest, envy. They were wearing nice suits, carrying leather briefcases and strolling in and out of the office throughout their busy days filled with customer appointments. That was the life I wanted!

Well, good things come to those who don't wait, so I started picking up the phone, dialling customers… and getting appointments! I soon worked on getting my health and life insurance agent accreditations, and then, with very little skill or experience, I just went out there and started trying to help people.

Four years later, I found myself married, living in a

foreign country (Scotland) and working as an IT consultant for a small private software testing company in the UK (once again, I secured this particular employment with no relevant technical skills at hand; I just wheedled my way in.)

A recession hit and we started losing some work; some consultants' projects were terminated early and they were put 'on the bench.' That's never a good thing in terms of job security, so I picked up the phone and started making sales calls. I had no idea what I was doing; I probably had no idea what I was even saying while I was saying it. But I started getting appointments and even some sales. What I didn't know at the time was how little I knew. Nobody was really guiding me or mentoring me, so I just had to find my own way. And I found myself in an environment of other salespeople who were also just finding their way. There was no system and very little in the way of training or education (nobody told me to read a sales book – if they had, I would've done it!)

Having coached over 100 growing businesses in the past 11 years, I have come across countless sales managers, sales directors and salespeople who are either failing miserably or, at best, just getting by. All those years ago, I found myself in that same situation. My clients were frustrated, and the salespeople were frustrated. Worse, salespeople were getting fired and then getting replaced by equally bad salespeople. Everybody wanted to do a good job; they just didn't know what to do.

I love sales. I love helping people. This job should be fun and rewarding in a thousand different ways. By writing this book, I wanted to take what is often taught in an overly complicated way and make it really simple. Easy to understand, easy to implement and easy to measure. I wanted the book to be short so that you could read it several times over, each time taking some new action or strategy and adding it to your toolkit.

Selling isn't easy and it shouldn't be easy. Salespeople should be some of the highest-paid people in a company and perhaps even the hardest working. But the highest performers and the highest earners should be the ones who dedicate the time to honing and perfecting their craft. And that's my aim here – that you will take some simple strategies and learnings from this short book and create a process or system that works for you.

And don't forget – have fun along the way. Enjoy the journey. Don't wait until you have success. If you're enjoying yourself now and loving what you do, success will come more quickly.

I hope you will get in touch and let me know how this book has positively impacted your results and your life.

Andrew Goldberg

November 2021

Introduction

Hitting Rock Bottom

I pull up about 200 metres away from my prospect's office, on the main road. Thankfully, there is plenty of on-street parking. I take a quick look around to see whether I need to pay for the privilege of leaving my car there for a couple hours. Nope, I'm good to go.

There are lots of spaces just outside their office, but I don't want to park there. I'm 30 minutes early and the last thing I need is for my prospect or anybody else in the company to see me sitting outside for ages before my scheduled appointment as if I have nothing better to do.

I certainly don't want them to see my pathetic Toyota family car. Bought used.

Most importantly, I don't want them to see what I'm about to do.

I switch the engine off and open the windows a crack – it's raining lightly, an uncharacteristic event in Scotland of course. I take out my mobile phone, open the notes section and go straight to the one entitled 'Prospect meeting affirmations.'

I look around to make sure no one's close by, take a deep breath, stare into the rear view mirror and loudly begin to make my case….

'I am a great salesperson! I am a great businessperson! I am assertive! I am knowledgeable! I am confident! I add value to my customers! I am a problem solver! I am a great leader! I am focused! I am part of the solution! My customers can't wait to meet me! I am well on my way to becoming the leading salesperson in my organisation! I have made lots of sales in the past, and I will make lots more sales in the future! I will make a sale today!'

I repeat these affirmations at the top of my lungs several times, then I check the clock. Three minutes have passed, and there are now 27 left to go before my appointment. I review my meeting notes again, which passes another few minutes. Then I listen to the car radio until it's time to find a closer parking space and head in.

That was my pre-sales meeting ritual for three years.

After the meeting, having shaken hands with the customer and smiled a friendly goodbye to the receptionist, I head out to my car in a daze. When I arrive home, my wife doesn't ask me how it went. She used to, but now she knows it's best to leave it alone. I'll tell her if I want to. Today I decide I want to talk; it's better than silence.

'I really think this one's going ahead. He absolutely loved what

I've got to sell and we got along really well – we both love the same films and he's even been to my hometown in America, so there was lots of rapport! There is a genuine need and they've got plenty of money, so there was no price objection either. He just wants a few days to think about it; he promised to get back to me. But it's an absolute no-brainer.'

'*That's great, hon,*' she says with a smile on her face. She doesn't ask any more questions.

She knows the truth and so do I, because this has been my *post*-meeting ritual for the past 44 sales meetings! I'd made no sales in four months. Zero. Nada. I had no money, I had no confidence and I had no idea what I was doing. In all honesty, I was ready to quit sales forever.

But it wasn't that simple! This wasn't just a job I could quit in the hopes of finding a better one. I couldn't just do what I'd done in the past and blame my employer, their product or the customer. This was *my* business and *my* responsibility. I owned it. I couldn't just leave! I had to figure out a way to make some sales and quickly! If not, I was likely to lose everything.

After weeks of chasing, I realised that particular sale would never materialise. That's when I finally bit the bullet and hired a business coach. When I first met with him, I was very honest. I told him I'd made no sales in my first four months of business. That's a 0% conversion rate. I had no money and no confidence, and I was embarrassed about my attire, my car and my presentation. I was at my wits end, desperate for him to tell me what was going wrong.

My coach listened to me intently, smiling empathetically. He understood. And he said to me the words I needed to hear: '*I can help you. Your results and your life are going to change, starting today.*'

And, suddenly, just like that, I felt relief and excitement. In fact, a whole flood of emotions started to pump through me and we hadn't even made any changes yet! It's remarkable how much power there is in just reaching out to somebody and asking for help.

As a starting point, he asked me to send him a few recordings of my recent sales meetings. Of course, like any good salesperson, I recorded my sales meetings, listened back to them and did analysis reports on all of them.

At our second coaching session, he gave it to me straight.

'Okay, Andy, I had a few hours in the car the other day while heading to a client and I listened to one of your sales meetings. At one point, I nearly drove off the road in shock because of what I was hearing.'

Don't pull any punches, I thought. The one he had listened to was three hours long! I remembered it well. The company had sent three representatives, and I felt outnumbered and a little overwhelmed. Nervous about their reaction to my opening pitch, I had latched on to my flipchart, frantically drawing all sorts of diagrams to teach them about the product in a desperate attempt to show them how much I knew and how impressive I was. In the throes of my panic, focusing stubbornly on my task, I'd entirely lost connection with the other people in the room. This meeting was a train wreck. All I could think was, *why did my coach have to choose that one to listen to?!*

'Do all the sales meetings go that same way?' my coach asked.

'They all begin differently, depending on what the customer needs and who they are. But, then, something happens. After my opening pitch, the customer asks a question or seems to push back and my heart sinks. It's happening again, *I think,* I'm losing them. *I can feel the rising anxiety and something primal kicks in. I stop listening to their concerns and start to attack on instinct, throwing a barrage of information their way to fill the gaps and prevent any further objections. I talk at a million miles an hour, without a pause, whether it's relevant or not, in order to protect myself from another failure. Ironically, it has the opposite effect. When it's over, I have no idea what's happened; I don't know what I've said or why I've said it. At the end of the meeting, dazed and confused, the customer shakes my hand and I leave as quietly and professionally as when I arrived.'*

Quiet understanding exudes from my coach's slightly pitying expression, and then he says the words that literally changed mine and my family's life:

'Okay, here's what I want you to do. Switch on your phone's recording device, because I want you to get this word for word. I'm going to tell you exactly what to say in your next sales meeting, and you're going to say it exactly like this, word for word.'

And then he spoke for an hour. I listened. I took notes.

I recorded. And, when he finished, I cried. Right there in the coaching session. I'm not kidding. I had my head in my hands, sobbing like a baby.

Why was I crying? Because I suddenly remembered all the dozens of failed sales meetings that I had been in and everything I had said and done when the panic had set in and I'd lost myself to fear. In other words, it suddenly hit me what had been going wrong all this time: I had been – and sorry if you're eating lunch right now – spewing what I once heard referred to as 'verbal diarrhoea' all over my customers. I had been going in without any system or script; without any idea at all as to what I was going to say. More importantly, I had mistakenly believed I needed to prove to them what a big shot I was in order to gain their trust. I came in ready to brag when they had concerns; to show these guys how much I knew, how smart I was, how bulletproof my product was, how long my company had been around and how many offices we had around the world.

I cried because of all the other 'remedies' I had tried, in desperation, to fix my sales slumps but had failed to get to the nub of the issue. Going on all the sales webinars and training courses. Changing my clothes and appearance to see if that would help. Smiling more. Smiling less. Getting customers to come to my office instead of the other way around. Nothing helped. Nobody helped. People were *trying* to help, but all the solutions they were throwing at me just made me feel more and more helpless. I kept trying stuff that worked for other people but it just didn't work for me.

I cried because of all the sales I had lost and for all the money I had left on the table. And I cried because my coach had showed me just how simple it was to change. Maybe not easy, but simple. I had completely missed it. Sales is a *process*. It requires a script and a series of simple, pre-determined steps that I actually knew like the back of my hand. Most importantly, this process can be easily measured, so we know that, as soon as any part of it stops working, we can immediately stop and make the necessary changes.

When the sobbing died down to just a whimper, my coach continued. He said, '*Okay, now I want you to take the recording, transcribe it if you need to, and memorise it, word for word. Then you're going to practise it out loud, again and again. Not just to yourself in a mirror, but you're going to practise it with your wife. You're going to practise it with your kids. You're going to practise it with the dog. You're going to practise it with a tree.*' (I'm not making this up; it's all there in the recording!)

And that's what I did. I learned my script word for word, and the very next week, at my very next appointment, I closed the sale! I walked away with an actual cheque for over six thousand pounds. And I've walked away with many more since then. In fact, 11 years on, I have a respectable sales conversion rate of over 70%, and it continues to rise. And, a few small changes aside, I use the exact same script today.

How Will This Book Help You?

Years after that meeting with my coach, I still remember the importance of that realisation. Looking back, I can see what a turning point it was for me in my work and in my life as a whole. Now, as a coach myself, I want to provide you with that same moment of truth and clarity. That script he gave me demonstrated the power of systems. I've since built my own approach based on these simple principles, and I want to help you create your own that will drive your future success.

So, what *is* a system? Simply put – and we love simple – a system is a series of steps, processes or scripts that are implemented and used consistently by all users, every time, to ensure consistent and positive results. A system in its simplest form is a checklist: you complete each item on the list and check it off as you do. When all the items are checked, you've completed the system and you will get the desired results. That's the idea – and it works!

The purpose of this book is to take your product, service, company, message, and value, and turn it into a simple system. A process that you simply need to learn and run each time.

Once we've developed your system, I want you to use it as a checklist. Take the book with you to sales meetings.

When coming up with the concept for this book, I pictured myself sitting in my car, pre-appointment, outside a prospect's office. Only this time, instead of shouting pointless affirmations into the mirror, I'm going through my checklist. Do I know what their number one pain point is? Did I confirm their budget? Am I meeting with the decision-makers? Have they been pre-framed? Have they read my testimonials? Now I can go into the appointment with confidence, and confidence always wins! You will be armed and ready with exactly what you are going to say, how you are going to say it and the belief that you will be handed that cheque at the end of the meeting.

The way I chose to structure this book was borne out of frustration with the well-intentioned people that were trying to help me in my sales journey. They challenged my mindset by getting me to do (what I thought at the time were) pointless exercises such as affirmations, listening to recordings of sales calls and studying NLP (neurolinguistic programming). While these are all useful tools in their own way, I just wanted to scream: *'Can somebody please just tell me what to do? Give me a checklist and I'll work through each point diligently! Give me a script and I will say the words!'*

I'm sure many of you have felt the same way. My aim here is to do just that. I want to turn your selling process into a foolproof system, so you are absolutely clear about what boxes need to be ticked, what questions need to be asked and what order your process should take. I've covered all the key elements in a typical selling situation: whether it's qualifying decision-makers, enquiring about budget, pricing and negotiations, asking for the sale or overcoming objections. Not every detail will apply to every sales situation, but I hope the structure of the book gives you a clear bird's eye view of the entire sales lifecycle, with the underlying principles easily accessible as you dig down into the areas that are most important for you right now.

How Should You Use This Book?

Ultimately, I want this book to achieve one particular outcome for you: a better sales conversion rate. That is, the percentage of sales you get from the number of appointments, leads, proposals and presentations that you conduct. In other words, I want you to get more sales for the same or less effort.

However, how you *use* the book is up to you. I have read many sales books (and so should you), and lots of them dictate to me *how* I should use the book. How's this for a plan? *I'll* decide how to use the book! I'll read it, and if it's very good, maybe I'll read it again with a highlighter pen. I'll implement the stuff I like and the rest will get absorbed into my subconscious.

So, I don't want you to feel there is a right or wrong way of doing this. Use the book as you like. Implement what you think will work for you and test and measure that. Allow the rest to soak in, and along with all the other books you read, this learning will encourage your development and growth as a salesperson.

Having said that, the design of the book is meant to resemble a checklist, and there are some key elements of any sales process that most, if not all, salespeople must implement if they want to achieve maximum effectiveness and conversion.

There are three other points to keep in mind. First, this book assumes you can get appointments or prospects in the first place. This is not a marketing or lead generation book. I could teach you how to cold call or get appointments but that's another book for another day.

Second, this book assumes that you sell a quality product or service, that it solves customers' problems or adds values to their lives and that you believe in its value. No sales strategy can help you become a great salesperson if you have a bad product.

Third, I would never tell you to stop doing the things that are working for you. Developing a sales process is about evolution, not revolution. If something has been effective for you, please keep doing it! Don't be afraid to make minor adjustments to the things that have been working, but remember to measure those adjustments and go back to the way things were if needed.

PART 1:

Foundations:
The Salesperson's Toolkit

Introduction

Before diving straight into the checklist, we need to make sure we've got the fundamentals right. No sales system in the world is going to help you if you don't have the right mindset around learning. You also need to start with the right attitude to selling, and you need to understand what a good salesperson is on this earth to do.

So, the first section of this book briefly discusses what I believe are the most important foundational concepts that any great salesperson must understand in order to make the checklist that follows work effectively.

In the pages that follow, I will make sure you've got your 'learning head' on; in other words, that you're ready to feel uncomfortable and prepared to try new things that may not work the first time. We'll discuss the importance of testing different methods and approaches, as well as tracking and measuring their effectiveness so we know whether what we're doing is actually working.

Remember, our results our determined by our actions and behaviours, but our actions and behaviours are determined by our mindset and our foundations. I know you're eager to get stuck in to the checklist, so I've kept Part 1 brief; but don't skip it!

Achieving Unconscious Competence as a Salesperson

By opening this book, you have demonstrated that you want to learn something new to improve your conversion rate and sales results.

However, we know that learning isn't always that straightforward. When we've learned something new, particularly something that we're excited about, we can't wait to go back to work and get started. But what happens then? Sure, you know; we've all been there. It doesn't work the first time. We're terrible at it. We don't get the response from the customer that we were hoping for or expecting. We are then faced with a few choices: do we try it again (the same way), do we try it again (in a different way) or do we give up entirely? Think back to the last time you learned something new, either from a book, a seminar, a podcast or a trainer.

Perhaps you attempted it but it didn't work quite the way you were hoping. What did *you* do? This is the challenge we always face when we grow and evolve.

Well, I know that life isn't that easy and you have to work hard to improve. Sales certainly isn't that easy; if it was then everybody would be doing it and we'd all be rich. So, my aim is to help you become a better salesperson by offering you *self*-help, not *shelf*-help. Shelf-help is when you read the book, you embrace the ideas, you get super motivated to try them out the next day at the office, and then, as soon as you come across resistance, you lapse straight back into old habits. Perhaps they don't work as you hoped, or perhaps you're just plain terrible at them. Perhaps, when you begin to try them out, you're so far out of your comfort zone that you immediately abandon the idea and go back to what you're comfortable with (even though that hasn't been getting you the results you wanted).

Does this sound familiar? Why don't we take a few moments to look at what is really going on when we go through the learning process and why it's so hard to keep going through those early stages.

There are four stages to the learning process that build upon each other:

1. Unconscious incompetence
2. Conscious incompetence
3. Conscious competence
4. Unconscious competence

At the start of every learning journey, we begin with what we call 'unconscious incompetence,' which essentially means you don't know what you don't know. In the case of sales, for instance, there are probably challenges that you didn't realise were getting in your way all this time. You didn't even know they existed, let alone the solutions required to address them.

Let's take a completely different example: learning to drive a car. As a child, you probably never knew that in order to drive a manual transmission car, you have to operate a clutch with your left foot or that you can only lift the clutch up at a certain speed, and to a certain point, or else you might stall the car. As a child, all you see is a grownup shifting the gears up and down like a race car driver. You are unconsciously incompetent at driving: there are things you don't know how to do, and you don't even know that you don't know them.

The second stage to learning is called 'conscious incompetence.' This is when you discover, either from somebody else or through your own study, that you don't know how to do something. Now you are at least *aware* that you don't know how to do it. A strategy may be presented in this book that you have never heard of before, and you will instantly be plunged into conscious incompetence. If a grownup shows a child all that's involved in operating a clutch, that child still won't be able to operate a clutch, but they'll now be aware that there is more to driving than meets the eye.

So, how do we feel during this second stage of conscious incompetence? Most likely we feel uncomfortable. Sometimes, it's horrible knowing that we don't know how to do something that we'd like to. It means we're going to have to do some hard work, some new learning, or even worse, some getting it wrong until we get it right. It looks hard and overwhelming. This is why, as I mentioned above, we often get stuck in shelf-help mode and retreat back to what we know when new ideas prove tricky to implement. Hopefully, though, we can take a more positive approach to this stage as well. We can be excited about the possibilities. By realising that there is something still to learn that could possibly improve our results, we are motivated to get stuck in.

Once we do commit to this process, however painful, we'll eventually move to the third stage of learning, which is called 'conscious competence.' Now, after a period of learning, we know *how* to do it but we have to *think* about it while we're doing it. It takes focus and effort, because we are still quite new to it. Think back to when you first started driving a car. You probably reviewed a lot of your knowledge, moment to moment, to ensure you were following the rules. You checked all your mirrors before pulling out, you'd think about how early to indicate left or right and you considered how far back to stay from the car in front of you. And, if you were like me, you were definitely thinking about how to operate the clutch every time you shifted gears!

But how do you drive now? If you've been driving for a while, you are probably in the fourth stage of learning: 'unconscious competence.' This means that you have been doing it for so long, and you are so good at it – or at least comfortable with it – that you don't even think about it while you're doing it. All of the processes we need to carry out occur automatically and instinctively – we can happily carry on a conversation with a passenger while indicating and changing lanes, for example. Ultimately, this is where we all want to get to, but we have to advance through the previous three stages first. At the beginning, in order to work our way through, we have to go on a voyage of discovery and ask some good questions so we can identify what we are incompetent of. We must then step out of our comfort zone and address those incompetencies until such time that we have achieved competence. Then we practise, practise and practise some more, until we are unconsciously competent.

If unconscious competence is the fourth and final stage of learning, then where do we go from there? Well, I'm glad you asked. We have to go back to conscious incompetence! In other words, we ask the question, "What *else* don't I know?" If we want to keep improving ourselves, then we have to keep going back to the start and identifying what else we are incompetent at. And remember how we feel during conscious incompetence: uncomfortable. So, be ready for the discomfort and embrace it. Seek it out. If we're uncomfortable, then that's an indication we are trying new things, learning new skills and growing.

As you work your way through this book, keep in mind that it's okay to feel uncomfortable. It's natural to go away and try something you liked and find that it didn't work the first time. Keep trying. Practise it. Change it up a little bit and try again. But, there's an art to this process. In order to keep moving forward, we need to test and measure. It's only through this process that we can ascertain what's working best for you and what isn't. Let's dive into this approach in a little more detail.

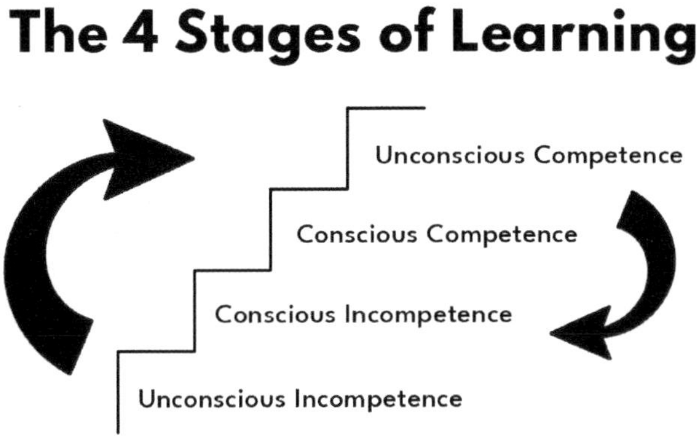

Figure 1: The Four Stages of Learning

The Importance of 'Test and Measure' in Making Progress

When you are my coaching client, or the client of any of the thousand-plus ActionCOACHes around the world, you will hear these three words – 'test and measure' – so often that you will want to scream. So, why do we drive you crazy by constantly repeating this mantra?

Simply put, you cannot improve what you do not measure. If you make some changes to the way you do things in response to this book and your results improve, that's great! However, you need to ask yourself: do you really know what caused the improvement? And, if you made more than one change, how do you know *which* change caused the improvement? Heady on success, but without the relevant data, you could easily attribute your results to the wrong thing and end up pursuing that to the detriment of your long-term success while ignoring the real game-changer.

Here's a real-life example from my early years in sales. At one point, early in my career, I decided to create a bit of an upheaval in the way I did things, mainly to see what would happen. I made four fundamental changes to my sales process:

1) I changed my attire. Instead of wearing a suit – the stereotypical, awfully outdated blue suit, white shirt and red tie – I began wearing business casual;
2) Instead of visiting clients at their offices, I asked clients to come to my office;
3) Knowing I'm a morning person, I insisted that all my sales appointments be scheduled for the morning; and
4) I made a few changes to how I introduced myself at the start of each meeting. For example, I would take three minutes to introduce myself instead of five. I would tell a personal story, whereas previously maybe I refrained from telling a personal story. And so on.

So, what happened? You guessed it. My conversion rate went up. Great! But which of the changes I made caused the improvement? Was it one of these things, some of them or the combination of all of them? What if bringing clients to my office was what really helped, but my change in attire was actually damaging. My conversion rate could have improved even more dramatically had I begun bringing clients to my office while leaving my attire the way it was. I didn't know, and I would never know until I began testing and measuring.

There is only way to do that. You need to change *just one thing* at a time, measure the impact and then act on the results. What would that look like in practice? I might change my attire and leave everything else the same, measuring my conversion rate over a period of, say, six weeks. Did my conversion rate go up or down, or did it stay the same? At the end of the measuring period, I can make some judgements about the impact of changing my attire and decide whether to retain that change or not. Next, let's begin scheduling all my sales appointments for the morning, while keeping everything else the same. Depending on the results at the end of the measuring period, I can now determine whether the time of day has any impact, positive or negative, on my ability to sell.

Another way to use test and measure to improve your approach is to break down the sales process into its constituent parts so you can see where the problems are. To do this, you may want to measure multiple conversion rates that exist in your sales process, beyond the obvious lead-to-sale default. For instance, you may look at your conversion rate of lead-to-appointment. That is the percentage of leads generated – say, for example, you've spoken to a decision-maker – that resulted in an appointment booked. You also have a conversion rate of appointment-booked-to-appointment-held. This would be highly relevant if you know that not all of your booked appointments end up going ahead. By knowing this more specific conversion rate, you can more easily analyse what is really happening at this stage of the sales process, i.e. is it about keeping the customer interested and excited about the appointment they booked with you, or is it about being more targeted and focused on the type of customers you are booking appointments with in the first place.

Let's take an example. Perhaps an important part of your sales process is a presentation to the customer. You've been measuring the conversion rates of lead-to-appointment booked and appointment-booked-to-appointment-held, which have been strong. Now you measure presentation-to-sale. If this conversion rate is low, then you will know that something is going wrong at the presentation stage. It's your presentation style or content that needs improving if you want to increase your overall sales conversion rate.

ActionCOACH founder and chairman, Brad Sugars, tells a great story from one of the many businesses he's owned over the years. In this women's clothing shop, their conversion rate was lower than they would like; specifically, the conversion rate of customers coming into the shop to customers buying clothes. Let's say it was around 15%. They then broke down their sales process into steps and started measuring the individual conversion rates. They quickly discovered that the conversion rate from customers who tried on clothing in the changing room to customers buying clothing was very high, let's say 70%.

If you were armed with this information, what change would you make to the sales process? That's right! Brad had his sales team make one very simple but hugely impactful change: instead of the sales assistants trying to sell clothes to the customers, or more likely just being helpful sales assistants, they began focusing their efforts on getting customers *into* the changing rooms. *'Just get them to try on clothes.'* was their new mantra, on the premise that there was a 70% chance they would buy something when they came out. It worked, of course, because the numbers never lie, but they would never have known to implement such an effective strategy had they not measured the different conversion rates at each step in their sales process.

I want to sum up this section by re-emphasising the importance of testing and measuring everything that you do. First, remember that whatever we measure tends to improve on its own because whatever we focus on tends to receive the support it needs to grow. Secondly, what works for you in one sales situation may not work for somebody else in another sales situation. Only by measuring the various aspects of our sales activity – not just the end results, but the activities leading up to the results – can we know what's working, what needs more focus, what needs to stop and what needs to change.

Know your numbers, always. You'll thank me for it later.

Becoming the Right Kind of Salesperson

'I Hate Salespeople'

Yes, that's right, you heard me. Actually, I didn't say it, but my new coaching client – let's call her 'Sue' – did. Sue was the owner of a building and construction company, which desperately needed to increase their sales. The problem was, Sue was doing all the selling herself. For years she knew she needed to hire professional salespeople but kept putting it off. Sue's own conversion rate was around 5%. In other words, she was putting in lots of effort for very little reward.

'*How come you haven't hired anyone?*' was the first question I asked.

'Because I hate salespeople.'

Truth be told, I had a pretty good idea of what she was going to say next.

'I have to deal with salespeople all the time in my business,' Sue explained. *'When they are selling to me, they only ever seem interested in talking about their product or their company. How long they've been in business, how much they care, how wonderful they are and how great their product or service is. They're pushy, they won't take no for an answer, and they don't listen.'*

'Go on…?'

'Worst of all, when we ask them if they can move on price, they do! That means the original price they quoted me wasn't their actual price. They were just trying to get as much money out of me as they could. When they lower their price for no real reason, that means I can't trust them. Or, it means they're desperate for business and are willing to discount just to win the sale. For once, I'd like a salesperson to stand by their pricing. I'd like them to be able to demonstrate, with confidence, why they charge that price point, or why they charge more than their competition and why I should still go with them."

'I hear you,' I said.

She's not alone. Lots of people hate salespeople for the same reasons. The truth is that there are lots of bad salespeople out there and there have been since the birth of, well, sales. There are, in all honesty, lots of ways to get it wrong and repel the very people we are trying to entice. Breaking it down, let's look at four different types of salespeople that we often see, day-to-day, and how to avoid making the common mistakes that Sue encountered.

The Four Types of Salespeople

The next time you are buying something or you encounter a salesperson, consider how they approach the process. You'll find that salespeople can be broken down into four distinct categories. It might be a good idea for you to think about which one you currently are as we go through this process. The important thing is to be brutally honest with yourself. Don't worry if you fall into one of the less-than-optimal categories; that's what we're here to fix!

Type 1: The Order Taker

The Order Taker does what it says on the tin. They have no interest in what you're looking for or what problem you're trying to solve. They may not even have a passable knowledge of their own products. They are only there to tell you how much something costs, bag it up for you and tell you to have a nice day.

I suppose, in an ideal world, where the product we sell is desperately wanted by everyone and customers will knock down our doors just to get it, this approach would work just fine. We would not need to do very much at our end, other than regularly raise our prices. But, of course, that is not the real world; being an order taker is not professional, nor does it move us towards a lifelong relationship with a new customer.

Type 2: The Product Pusher

Quite the opposite of the Order Taker, the Product Pusher loves to talk about their product and company ad nauseum. They know all about the features and benefits, and they can't wait for you to stop talking so they can launch into their spiel. It's their one man (or woman) show and you are an afterthought. Your needs are far down their list of priorities. As you are standing there listening to them go on and on with unfettered enthusiasm about how wonderful they are, what is the Product Pusher doing? Basically, feeding their own ego.

The Product Pusher thinks you care about the colour or the chrome finish of their product. They think you care about all the accessories it comes with. They think you care that they've got seven offices dotted around the country and have been in business since 1993. Unfortunately, they don't have the empathy to pick up on what you actually care about. They don't listen and they don't ask questions.

Type 3: The Over Seller

The Over Seller will tell you whatever they think you need to hear in order to win the sale. They have been trained to the point of brainwashing to sell the living hell out of their products, knowing that they will be able to convince – notice I said 'convince' rather than persuade – you to succumb to their charms and excitement, and ultimately, make a purchase. Like the Product Pusher, they don't listen and they don't let you get a word in edgeways. And, worst of all, they will lie, make promises they don't actually believe they can fulfil and exaggerate their capabilities. Once the sale is complete and the Over Seller has departed, they generally do not mind whether you are happy with their purchase or not. If the sale has gone through, they feel they have done their job.

Type 4: The Problem Solver

And, finally, there is the Problem Solver. The one type of salesperson that helps the customer find what they actually need. Their mission is to find out exactly what is going to be the best possible solution for you. They are focused on you, the customer, and not themselves, their product or their company. Once you have implemented the systems laid out in this book, you too, will be a problem solver!

So, let's go back to Sue. She *thinks* she hates all salespeople, but she doesn't. She only hates types 1-3. The problem is that most salespeople fall into these first three categories, so that's her only experience when it comes to interacting with salespeople. If Sue's salespeople and vendors were all Problem Solvers, would she ever have uttered the words, 'I hate salespeople'? Of course not. Sue would be surrounded by people whose mission was to *solve Sue's problems*. Sue would love salespeople.

So, which type are you? Whatever the answer is, don't worry. By the end of this book, you will be a type 4 Problem Solver, because your new sales system will be created specifically around the mission of solving customers' problems.

So, How Do You Become a Problem Solver?

If you want to be a Problem Solver, and you're going to get Sue to *love* you rather than *hate* you, then you will need to identify exactly what the problem is that your product or service actually solves. What is driving your customers through your doors? Or, if you are doing outbound marketing strategies, why are customers taking your call or agreeing to meet with you in the first place? Let's be clear: it's not because they love your product or service, because they like spending time with salespeople or because they are bored.

It's because they have a problem.

It could be a negative problem. For example, they might be short-staffed which is causing them to let their customers down. Their garden may be growing out of control and they don't have the necessary tools to clean it up. Or they may suddenly need wheelchair access into their house which they hadn't needed in the past.

Alternatively, it could be a good problem. When a customer has a pain point, it doesn't mean they are sad or frustrated or sick. It just means there is a gap that needs to be filled, and they need a valuable resource or expert to fill it for them. They may have just received a significant promotion at work, and they want to use the extra money to enlarge their house and create the living space they've always wanted. Perhaps they've decided they want a new pet. Or maybe their business is evolving so fast that they need more help internally to keep up with the growth.

Your job is to find out what that problem is so you can offer a solution that meets their needs and wants *exactly*. You want to demonstrate to your customer that you are there to understand their problem as best you can. The way that you do this is by using a script. This is going to make up a large part of your new sales checklist. And the first thing we need to do in this script is to ask questions to identify the problem. We'll go into more detail on exactly what this looks like in Part 2 of the book. In the next section, however, let's consider not just *what* you need to ask your customer but *how* you need to ask them. Good communication, after all, is the hallmark of the Problem Solver.

Harnessing Your Customer's Communication Style

How do you communicate with your customers? What is your personality type and style of connecting with people?

Are you a natural people person? Do you love to laugh and chat and find out about other people? Do you like the spotlight and are you comfortable talking about yourself? Or are you more reserved, quieter and calmer? Are you an active listener rather than a constant chatterbox?

Are you more task-oriented or people-oriented? In other words, are your conversations more about the product or service you are selling, or do you focus your conversations on the customer and their life? Are you detail-oriented or big picture? For example, do you spend lots of time exploring all the facts and figures, or do you prefer to focus on the headlines so you can get quickly to the presentation and the sale? Do you like to stand close to people when you talk and make plenty of eye contact, or do you like to keep a bit of distance?

Most importantly, have you ever considered all of these questions before? If not, it might be time to start! One of the most important tools we can use to build better rapport with people is by better understanding their preferred method of communication and adapting our own communication style to theirs. In this way, we can build stronger relationships and persuade them to lean towards our way of thinking. It's all about understanding how to influence rather than dominate.

Neurolinguistic programming is a very popular method that is often used in sales training programmes to facilitate this understanding of people's communication styles and how best to harness them in order to connect with customers. At my company, ActionCOACH, we prefer a simpler system: DISC.

The Four Customer Categories and Their Communication Styles

People's behaviours and communication styles are complex, of course, and they change depending on context and circumstance. However, in general terms, people tend to fall into one of four categories:

- D – Dominance
- I – Influence

- S – Stability (or Steadiness)
- C – Compliance (or Conscientiousness)

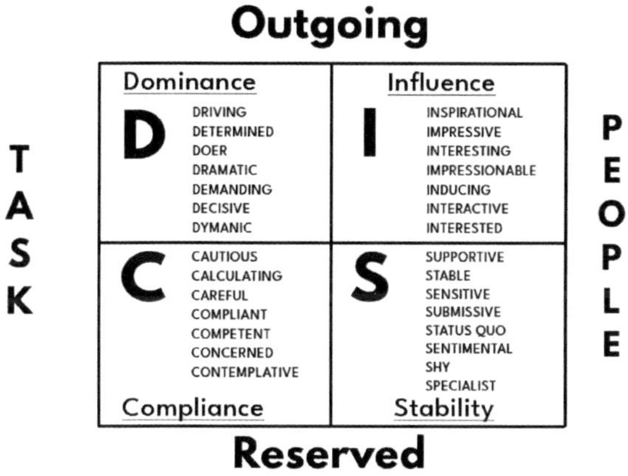

Figure 2: The Four Customer Categories

D = Dominance

'D' stands for dominant, directive, determined, dramatic, demanding, decisive, dynamic and a 'doer.' Dominant people – 'Ds' as we call them - are decision-makers and wield power. They are outgoing, competitive and they tend to exude confidence, and thus they respect confidence in others. Ds are less about the detail and more about the results. They don't need to know every little thing about your product and service. They just want to know whether it's going to solve their problem or not. If you spend too much time talking about the detail with a D, they will lose patience with you or you will lose their attention. They may even get bored and extricate themselves from the conversation!

Because Ds are task-oriented as opposed to people-oriented, you don't need to be their best friend. Don't spend a lot of time with chit-chat. You don't need to ask a D who their favourite sports team is or the ages of their kids. Get the rapport building out of the way as quickly as you can, and then get on with the sales process!

A word of caution when selling to a D: they will often try to gain control of the conversation by asking you questions and continually bouncing the ball back into your court. You need to maintain control by asking questions back. Think of it like a game of tennis.

So, when selling to a D, stick to the facts and the agenda. Show them results with confidence and they will buy from you.

I = Influence

'I' stands for influential, interactive, inspirational, impressive, interesting (and interested), impressionable and inducing. People who are predominantly an I in the DISC profile are outgoing and people-oriented. They are popular and might be known as a 'people person.' You will know the type; you may even be one. Influencers are the folk who love to be around other people. They make new friends quickly and often. When they're not hosting parties, you'll find them at other people's. They love to laugh, they love to talk about themselves and they love to hear about other people.

Like the Ds, Is are also confident decision-makers. However, their decisions will be made somewhat differently. The aim when selling to an I is to get them to like *you*, as opposed to liking the product. Or, at the very least, you need to get them to like you *before* you get them to like your product. If you achieve this, they are much more likely to buy from you.

Since Is love to laugh, get them laughing. Have a few good jokes or funny stories up your sleeve. Since Is love to talk about themselves, ask questions about them. Ask about their family, their home and their interests. However, let them do most of the talking as they like to hold court. Be warm and be interested in them. And, more importantly, be interest*ing*!

Selling to an I isn't complicated: just be likeable.

S = Stability

'S' stands for stability seeker, supportive, sensitive, sincere, submissive, sentimental, shy, specialist and seeker of the status quo. Like the Is, Ss are also people-oriented, although they are reserved and introverted rather than outgoing. The predominant characteristic of the S profile is that they have a high emotional intelligence. They are sensitive, sincere, friendly (in a quieter way than the Is) and understanding. Ss value relationships, and while they may have a smaller social circle than the Is, their relationships will likely be deeper and more meaningful. In other words, they probably have fewer Facebook friends but they'll actually know them all and be interested in them!

Since one of the primary characteristics of an S is that they are a stability seeker, they are likely resistant to change. They will take their time to make decisions, and generally, they will only do so once they trust you. It is therefore essential that you build rapport and trust with them from the outset. They don't need the same type of interaction as the I; in other words, you don't need lots of bubbly laughter and chatter. But you will need to offer plenty of eye contact, demonstrate good listening skills, understanding and empathy, and give them plenty of reassurance.

Guide an S from the start, telling them what you want them to do up front. Give them firm nudges in the right direction but never be pushy; you will lose their trust straight away. In fact, never be pushy with *any* customer please!

One final note about the S customer: if you are looking to get a 'decision on the day,' don't get your hopes up. Ss take the longest to close and, if you're going to win them round, you need to be okay with that. They need to feel they can trust you implicitly. Continue to build that relationship as a friend while showing them that you have their best interests at heart, and they will eventually become loyal customers for life!

C = Compliance

'C' stands for conscientious, cautious, calculating, compliant, competent, concerned and contemplative. This conscientious risk avoider is reserved, introverted and task-oriented. This means that, like the Ds that we discussed earlier, the Cs are also less focused on the people aspect of a conversation and more focused on the task at hand: the product, the service and the results. Cs tend to be analytical, precise and accurate. They may come across as serious, critical, defensive or fussy, but in fact, they simply want to make sure they have all the facts before making a decision. They need to know they are making the right choice and eliminating any risk. Cs are the ones who will ask themselves: 'What can go wrong?' It helps if you can predict what their fears might be in advance and try to address them before they've been raised.

Cs will be challenging, even distrusting, and will ask lots of questions. They are asking for a reason and you will need to give them all the answers they are looking for. Make sure you find the information they need to make a decision and be patient with them. They are not trying to be difficult, just careful.

Because they take a long time to make a decision, you may also need to follow up with them. To help them along in the process, you can ask them questions such as:

'What other information will you need to make your decision?'

'What else do you need to see from me?'

'What else can I show you?'

Provide the C with plenty of social proof which they will find compelling, such as testimonials, case studies and success stories. A guarantee will also be very valuable to them as it eliminates risk. Most importantly, give your C plenty of reassurance and alleviate all their fears.

How Will I Know Which Category My Customer Falls Into?

This is a valid question. There are assessment questionnaires that you can take online for a nominal fee to determine your own personality type and natural communication style, as well as those of your sales teams if you have them. But you can't exactly ask every one of your customers to sit down and take a 10-minute assessment before you begin, can you? But, if you don't know which category they fall into, how are you supposed to know how to best connect with them?

On top of that, the truth is that most customers have decided whether they like you enough to buy from you *within a few minutes* of meeting you! That's right: even if people don't realise it at a conscious level, you only have a short window to make the best possible impression on somebody when you first meet them. So, if I walk into your shop, you're going to need to figure out pretty darn quick that the last thing I want is for you to become my best friend before you begin selling to me.

So, how can you quickly figure out which of the four – D, I, S or C - your customer is? Or, in other words, their

DISC profile. Well, fear not! We've assembled a 'quick and dirty' cheat sheet below that you can use to swiftly categorise people based on simple observations. Remember, though, that human beings are complex. You cannot simply slap a letter on somebody and expect it to reveal exactly what is the best way to treat them or communicate with them. But we can, at the very least, make a fast and educated guess so that we can get off on the right foot. We can then continue to adjust our style accordingly as we get to know our customer better.

Identifying Your Customer's Communication Style: The Quick and Dirty Cheat Sheet

Here is the 'quick and dirty' method of identifying someone's basic communication style.

1. First, ask yourself this question: *Is this person outgoing or reserved?*

a. Outgoing people will likely exhibit the following behaviours or characteristics:

i. A fast talking pace.
ii More telling (than asking).
iii Talking at a louder volume.
iv. More inflection in their voice.

b. Reserved people will likely exhibit the following behaviours or characteristics:

i. A slower talking pace.
ii. More asking (than telling).
iii. Softer speech at a lower volume.
iv. A more monotone voice (less inflection).

2. Once you've identified whether the person is outgoing or reserved, which you should be able to do very quickly, you should next ask yourself the following questions, depending on the outcome of the previous question:

a. For outgoing people, ask yourself: *Is the person's behaviour more competitive and directing or more talkative and interactive?*

i. People who are more competitive and directing will exhibit the following behaviours or characteristics. These are your Ds:

1. A closed and more formal posture.
2. More focused on goals and results.
3. An inexpressive or cool face (i.e. they're not giving much away).
4. Focused on the 'what?' e.g. 'What does the product do?' 'What results will I get?' 'What does it cost?

ii. People who are more talkative and interactive will exhibit the following behaviours or characteristics. These are your Is:

1. An open and more casual posture.
2. More focused on people and approval.
3. An animated and warm face.
4. Focused on the 'who?' e.g. 'Who else works in your company?' 'How long have you worked for the company?' 'Who will be my account manager moving forward?' 'Who can I speak with if there's a problem?'

b. For reserved people, ask yourself: *Is the person's behaviour more accommodating and doing or more assessing and thinking?*

i. People who are more accommodating and doing will exhibit the following behaviours or characteristics. These are your Ss:

1. An open and more casual posture.
2. More focused on cooperation and stability.
3. A relaxed and warm face.
4. Focused on the 'how?' e.g. 'How does this work?' 'How can I be sure it will work?'

ii. People who are more assessing and thinking will exhibit the following behaviours or characteristics. These are your Cs:

1. A closed and more formal posture.
2. More focused on quality and analysis.

3. An inexpressive and cool face.
4. Focused on the 'why?' e.g. 'Why is it designed that way?' 'Why should I go with your product over somebody else's?' 'Why do you think this option is the best fit for me?'

Quickly identifying the communication style or DISC profile of a person you have just met takes practise but it's well worth it.

A word of caution: the most important skill of the salesperson is listening. While speaking with a new customer and trying to hold all of this information in your head, don't forget to be present with them and actively listen to what is being said. Using DISC or other NLP strategies is great, and it's important to take the leap to improve your skills, but not at the expense of hearing what the customer is saying.

Once you have identified their style, what then? Regardless of your natural communication style – whether you're outgoing or reserved, task-oriented or people-oriented – remember to communicate with your customer in the way *they* prefer to communicate, not the way *you* prefer to communicate. DISC expert, Tony Allesandra, and founder of Assessments 24x7, refers to this concept as the 'platinum rule.' Whereas the golden rule is: 'Do unto others as you would have done unto you,' the platinum rule states: 'Do unto others as they would have done unto them.' Sorry golden rule, but you got it wrong. If we simply treat others as we'd like to be treated, we are ignoring the specific personality traits and emotional and intellectual needs of the individual we are interacting with. We assume, wrongly, that they are just like us. This is not about being a fake or somebody you're not. It's about using simple methods to improve the art of communication and to get the best possible win-win result for you and your customer.

Let's take an example. Imagine my wife and I were out shopping. As somebody who is high up the D scale, if you employed all those old-school techniques of using my name 10 times, touching my elbow at least once (yes, some sales trainers really still teach that!) and asking me about my kids or where I'm from, you'll just annoy me. Just tell me what's going to be the best solution for me and why, tell me the price, and tell me quickly.

Try selling the same product to my wife, who is high up the S scale, and you'll need to take a totally different approach. You'll have to take your time, answer all her questions and give her plenty of reassurance that there is little to no risk. Most importantly, you must ensure that she trusts you implicitly if you want to win the sale. Customers similar to my wife ask salespeople lots of questions and take their time, less because they want all the information and more because they just want to feel comfortable with the situation: the salesperson, the company and the product. They want reassurance.

See the difference? You're not employing tricks or tactics, you're simply giving the customer the information they need in the style they are comfortable with to ensure they are primed to do business with you.

As I mentioned in the introduction, give yourself permission to be bad at this when you first try it, but keep at it and you will get better. You should start to notice quite quickly that your customers are responding well to you, offering you the responses you were looking for, and ultimately, saying 'yes' to you more often!

Conclusion

People buy from people they know, like and trust. But to different people, that means different things. You need to find out what information each individual customer wants and how they need it to be delivered to them, and quickly! Some will need you to be their best friend and others won't be a 'people person' at all, preferring to hear about the facts; some will want a lot of detail and others will just want to know what results they'll get; some will care about how trustworthy you are and others will only care how trustworthy the product is; some will take their time and others will make a decision on the day.

Using DISC or other communication style tools will enable you to adapt your communication and behaviours accordingly so that people are happy to do business with you. Only after the customer likes and trusts you will they agree to buy from you.

Your job is to know what type your customer is. It's time to stop communicating the way *you* prefer to, and start communicating the way *your customer* prefers to!

PART 2:

The Sales Meeting Checklist

Introduction

Alright, let's take a step back and breathe. We've covered some of the key fundamentals to being a great, problem-solving salesperson.

It's now time to take those fundamentals and apply them to a sales system – a checklist. The salesperson's job is to understand the customer's needs and ensure the sales process continues moving forwards towards a decision – hopefully a 'yes' decision!

In Part 2, I have created for you an 18-point checklist of the most important elements that you must consider throughout the sales process. Here we are going to cover, among other things, the importance of having a script, how to open a sales conversation, getting agreement from the customer all the way through the process, ascertaining budget and decision process, qualifying customers, checking to make sure you are on the right path as you guide the customer towards a solution and handling objections. We'll cover negotiation techniques, upselling, guarantees and social proof as well.

Once you've used this section to create or modify your own sales process, you can use this checklist as, well, an *actual* checklist. Use it while you're preparing for sales meetings and during the meetings themselves. Keep the checklist in front of you, in your notebook or in your car. And be a 'control freak' with your checklist: don't move the sales process on until you've ticked the necessary boxes at each stage.

Let's begin…

1

Have a Script: Practise, Practise, Practise

This is it. The #1 strategy to improve your sales conversion rate, no matter what business you're in. You'll notice that it's the first point on the checklist. That's because almost everything else we're going to cover needs to make its way into your script.

I'm sure a lot of you are thinking, *I don't want a script, because I will sound scripted. I hate when I get cold called and you can tell that the caller is using a script. It sounds false and robotic.* Yes, I hear you, and I have had the same experiences. But we're not going to sound false or robotic. When a script is written in the style that you would naturally speak in, using your own words, and you have practised it to the point where it feels genuine, you will not sound scripted. In fact, when you have truly reached 'unconscious competence' in your script, you will be able to step out of it when necessary, or jump ahead and then back again, or expand on something further when a customer asks you a question. The script should be written verbatim, but that doesn't mean that your every moment in that meeting will be scripted.

The script is there to ensure you stay grounded and focused on what's important, i.e. meeting the customer's needs and moving the sales process forward. The script prevents us from losing the thread and going on a tangent. It keeps us from panicking when the customer throws us a curve ball. It stops us giving too much information to the customer and confusing or overwhelming them. Perhaps, most importantly, a script gives us confidence. When we go into a sales meeting knowing what we're going to say and what we're going to ask, as well as how we're going to deal with the variety of situations that we might find ourselves in, we go in self-assured and relaxed. When we're confident in this way, the customer picks up on that and feels more comfortable buying from us. When we're relaxed, the customer relaxes, and they are more likely to open up to us about what they're really looking for and why.

Still not convinced? You will be by the time you get to the end of this section.

Let's start working on our script now.

2

Build Rapport: Establishing Your Relationship

Before we get stuck in, I am going to assume that you already have one essential skill in place: people skills. No sales book, strategy, script or method in the world is going to make you into a great or even a half-decent salesperson, if you are not likeable. As I said earlier, people buy from people they know, like and trust. The tools in this book will encourage people to trust you. However, you are on your own when it comes to 'know' and 'like'. For some recommended reading on those subjects, I would certainly begin with the old favourite, *How to Win Friends and Influence People*, by Dale Carnegie.

Having said that, no sales book would be complete if we didn't at least touch on the subject of likeability, so let me offer you four top tips to get you started:

1. **Get 'em laughing:** People love to laugh and have fun. And so it follows that people love to be around other people who are fun and make them laugh. '*But I'm not funny*,' I hear you say. Well, you better *get* funny. Enrol in a stand-up comedy class. There will be adult classes at your local college or university, or even online. Watch more comedy, read some funny books and record any stories or anecdotes about funny encounters and experiences you've had. Mostly, just look for funny; it's all around you when you tune into the absurdity of life. But, remember, be yourself and don't put on an act. Try to let it come naturally. Don't steal somebody else's jokes or comedy style. You'll get caught out in the end as being fake.

2. **Smile:** Smile a lot. Smile 'til it hurts. I'm not a natural smiler myself, I can tell you. I've got a condition known as R.B.F. If you're not familiar with that abbreviation then Google it. Smiling lets your customers relax. They'll like you more. They'll listen more attentively to what you have to say. And *you'll* feel more relaxed and confident too.

3. **Find commonality:** When all else fails, and – damn it – you're just not a funny, smiling, likeable chap or gal that day, then at the very least, be sure to find commonality with your customer. Find something, anything, that the two of you share. The discovery of

commonality, no matter how small or trivial, immediately forms a bond between people, resulting in a certain degree of trust and even, perhaps, friendship.

In order to find commonality, you might need to ask a few probing but casual questions before the official meeting starts. If the weather has been nice, perhaps ask how they prefer to enjoy the outdoors when the sun is out. Or try to find out about their local sports team and whether they are an avid fan. Just get conversational somehow. Imagine you were meeting at a dinner party instead of a sales meeting, and the ball was in your court to start a conversation. Have a few good conversation starters up your sleeve (figuratively of course, you'll need to memorise them). Can't think of any? Below are six examples of starter questions and statements that I've used in the last year. They all helped me to connect with my customer on a personal level before I jumped into the business pitch:

- What do you enjoy most about your work?
- What frustrates you the most about your work?
- Lovely office. Do you have a long commute?
- How did you get into this line of work anyway?
- I saw on your LinkedIn profile that you follow Richard Branson. How does he inspire you?
- Who else inspires you?

If all else fails, and you are meeting at the customer's place of business or their home, a good strategy to build rapport or find commonality is to do a really quick scan of your surroundings. Perhaps look for something on the wall such as a photograph or piece of art, or something on a table like an unusual trinket or book that you can enquire about. Preferably you want to choose something that you may be able to speak about with some experience or empathy. Bingo! Your commonality will be assured.

A word of caution: Once you found commonality, move on. Don't stay on the subject for very long. It's a way of connecting with your customer in the first instance, but you aren't friends and they'll start to feel awkward if you spend too long discussing personal issues. Ultimately, you are there in a business capacity.

4. **Use your customer's name as often as possible:** A person's name is their favourite sound. Using it makes the connection personal and they feel seen. It demonstrates that they are the most important person in the room. Make sure you're pronouncing their name correctly, and if you're not sure, ask. It's perfectly okay to ask somebody how to pronounce their name. It shows respect and demonstrates that you care about them and your future relationship. You can find audio pronunciations

of most names on the internet, so you can arrive prepared. If there is more than one customer in the room, be sure to learn all their names, and use them all at least once or twice.

Alright, so, you got them to like you! Some commonality has been found, their names have been used and some laughing or smiling has taken place. Let's get on with the script. Your customers will thank you for it.

As alluded to earlier, your primary job as a salesperson is to identify the pain point or problem that your customer wants you to solve, and that means you are going to have to ask some questions. Questions are the most important part of your script, indeed, the most important part of your entire sales process, and so we may have to ask quite a few. We may even need to dig quite deep to get to the 'real issue.' Let's consider how we start this process of questioning off in a way that will reassure and encourage your customer.

3

Use a Statement of Intent: Getting Your Customer on Board

We start off our script by asking for permission from the customer. This usually comes in the form of what we call an 'intent statement,' which explains what it is that you are going to do. You need to take control of the meeting and kick off the serious business of business with an opening line. Here is what I recommend, and I don't mean take it and make it your own; I mean, use it word for word:

'Just so I can help you best, is it okay if I ask you a few questions?'

Pretty simple, eh? Here's why I like this intent statement.

First, it signals that the time for rapport building is over and it's time to move on. This puts you in charge. In fact, whoever is asking the questions is in charge of any discussion. Why? Because when you ask a question, the other person has to answer. They are being directed by your prompts. You can then ask another question, thereby keeping control of the direction of the meeting.

Second, you are positioning yourself as someone who is there to help. Remember, all a customer really wants to know is how you are going to *help them* solve their problem.

Third, you are preparing them for what's going to happen in the meeting i.e. that you are going to ask them questions. And while most salespeople may ask one or two questions to get a quick idea of what your technical requirement is, you are going to ask more questions than them! You are going to dig deeper. Your customers need to know to expect this. You don't want them wondering: *What's going on? Why is this person interviewing me? Am I taking a survey?* By letting the customer know you are going to ask them lots of questions, and that the reason for this is to help them, they will relax and feel more comfortable with the process.

Your customer will say 'yes' to this opening question. They always do. Now we can begin asking the important questions.

4

Have an Objective: What Happens Next?

An Objective Moves Things Forward

Remember to have a clear objective or a desired outcome for any meeting or conversation you are going to have with a customer. The greatest benefit of goal setting, in any context – be it in business, fitness, relationships and so on – is that you are more likely to achieve a goal if you set one! And, while I know this sounds blatantly obvious, you'd be surprised at how often we don't do this.

Get out your highlighter pen and highlight this statement: *The job of the salesperson is to move the sales process forward.*

Every touch point with your prospect or customer – every phone call, video call, email and proposal – has a direct or indirect impact on your desired outcome i.e. a sale. And that makes every step of the sales process as important as the next. Any misstep at any point could be the thing that costs you the sale or causes a delay. Most likely, having a conversation or meeting with a customer *without* having a clear objective or purpose could result in wasted time and interrupt your momentum.

Thus, every action that you take with a customer should have a clear objective that works in favour of both you and the customer: you are moving closer towards a sale and your customer is moving closer towards getting the right (and best) solution for their needs.

I will always remember a quote from the great sales trainer John Costigan: *"I never do anything unless I know why I'm doing it."* That means that you never pick up the phone to chase a prospect until you're absolutely clear in your own mind what you want from the call. You never visit a prospect to deliver a presentation or proposal until you're absolutely clear about what you want to get at the end of it. In other words, you must already have it clear in your own head as to what the ideal 'next step' will be following the interaction.

Whatever your goal is for each interaction, it can probably best be summed up as wanting to further the relationship with the customer and move the sales process *forward.* One way of achieving this is by putting the ball in the customer's court as to the next steps. You focus on finding out from them - after the conversation, the meeting, the presentation or whatever interaction you have planned with your customer – *what happens next.*

What Happens Next?

These three words have completely revolutionised the way that I sell and dramatically improved my own results! By regularly and consistently asking the customer, '*Once we have done x, if it all goes well, what happens next?*' we ensure that we continually move towards a win-win situation. We move closer towards a sale, and the customer moves closer towards a solution. We are effectively asking the customer to make an agreement with us *before* we take the next action step.

Let's look at an example so that we can better illustrate this important concept. Let's say I have already had one or two exploratory conversations with a customer and we are at the point where we are scheduling our first, more 'formal,' face-to-face meeting. We've got the date in the diary, and perhaps even an agenda, but before I hang up the phone, I might ask this:

'Just before I let you go, Mr. Customer, can I just ask, if it all goes really well at our meeting next Thursday, and you really love what you hear, what happens next?'

You can always take the language and change it up a little to better suit your style. For example:

- *'What would be the next step?'*
- *'Where would we go from there?'*
- *'How would you want to move forward?'*

These are all possible variations of the same question, '*What happens next?*'

Whatever language you use, be sure to have an agreement with your customer about what happens next *before* each step occurs. A verbal contract if you will. I've sometimes heard this referred to in other books and sales training courses as a 'conditional close' or 'mini-close.' Now, I'm not a big fan of the word 'close,' because as you'll see later on in this book, closing is not necessary to get a sale. Many people see closing as a tactic or a trick to get the customer to say yes to something. We're not going to do that. On the other hand, we do want our customer continually saying yes to the next step or the next action. *I'm going to do something, and you're going to do something, so that we continue to move forward towards the best solution for you.* The more you get your customer saying yes during the sales process, the more accustomed they become to saying yes to you, and the more likely it will be that they say yes when you ask for the sale.

5

Understand Their Needs: It's all About the Questions

The Questioning Process

The bulk of your script will be made up of questions. In fact, questions are the most important part of your sales process. Why? Because sales is an *emotional* process, not a *logical* one. What do I mean by that? Well, a customer's decision to buy from you is based less on the product or service that you offer, where you are located, how long you've been in business and your price. A customer's decision is based much, much more on whether they like you, whether they trust you, whether this feels right, how badly they want to get their problem solved and how excited they are that they've found the person to solve it for them!

And, to get to that emotion, we ask questions. You'll see how this works as it unfolds.

Questions can be broken down into two types: emotional questions and logical questions. Logical questions are important, certainly. As a problem solver, you need to know exactly what your customer is looking for. You need to understand their problem, know their budget, be aware of their decision-making process and so on. But it's the emotional questions that are going to get underneath someone's skin and make them realise that you're the person they've been looking for all this time!

So, what questions should you ask? There are many good opening questions out there to choose from, but before you Google them (and you should), let me share mine with you:

'What made you decide to meet with me?'

This is a great starting question because it is quite directive. It is encouraging, if not forcing, the customer to get to the point of what they are looking for from you. It gets them thinking and talking about the problem they have, but it may also lead them towards explaining why they are considering you as opposed to the competition.

Now, here's your 'dig deep' question. Ask this one a lot. Ask this whenever you can't think of what else to ask. Most importantly, ask with a genuine desire to listen and understand. Then ask it again.

'Tell me more about that.'

Asking this question achieves three things. It will encourage the customer to give you more information about their problem and their feelings about it, which could be invaluable in gaining their trust and finding the right solution. It also allows them to feel listened to and prioritised in the conversation, which will put them in the right frame of mind. Finally, it stimulates the customer's emotions by reminding them why they are seeking out your product or service in the first place, making them more likely to 'want' to take action.

The greatest list of questions to ask in a sales meeting comes from Philip Hesketh's brilliant book, *Persuade*, in which Philip lists his 'top 50 questions of persuasion.' At the top of Philip's list are, in my opinion, the three best questions you can ask a customer, each of which is followed by, '*Tell me more about that.*'

1. What is the most important thing to you about…?

a. Tell me more about that.

2. What is the most frustrating thing to you about…?

a. Tell me more about that.

3. What are your expectations exactly?

a. Tell me more about that.

To ensure you don't sound like a broken record, you will need to change it up now and again, with alternatives to, '*Tell me more about that*' such as, '*Why?*' or, '*Why is that?*' or, '*Of all the things you could have said to answer my question, why did you choose that one?*'

Hopefully, by this stage, you are getting a good idea of what your customer is looking for and how you are going to solve their problem. I'll bet you're just dying to get to the bit where you get to present your solution and demonstrate your expertise! Well, we're not there yet. We're going to ask *even more* emotional questions.

Emotional questions come in two categories: pain and vision. Pain questions focus on the problem and its negative impacts:

- *How long has this been going on?*
- *What else have you tried to fix the problem?*
- *Why are you looking to solve the problem now? What has stopped you from fixing the problem before?*
- *What would be the impact on your life/business/family/etc. if you didn't fix the problem?*
- *How much is this problem costing you financially and emotionally?*
- *Did you expect this would ever happen or that you would ever find yourself in this situation?*
- *How much longer can you last without doing something?*

Conversely, vision questions focus on the beneficial outcomes of solving their problem:

- *What would be the impact on your life/business/family/etc. if you were to solve this problem?*

- *How will you feel once the problem has been solved/the product is in your home/you've taken possession of …?*
- *What would this look like?*
- *What does your ideal situation look like?*
- *What does the ideal solution look like in your mind?*

And then, as always, you can follow these questions with, '*Tell me more about that.*'

Above all, remember what the customer really wants to know over everything else: their WIIFM. WIIFM stands for: '*What's in it for me?*' and this is what customers really care about. Imagine you're explaining to your customer that you have five offices dotted around the country and you've been in business since 1991. The customer is thinking: *Big deal. How does this help me?* While you're composing your sales script, keep this acronym in the forefront of your mind. Whenever you add something new to the script, ask yourself, *What's in it for the customer? Why do they care?* It is an effective and simple method for testing whether what you are about to add to your sales process is going to add value to the customer and help them make the best buying decision. The golden rule is: if there's nothing in it for the customer, don't say it!

It's a Conversation, Not an Interview

Your script is all about the questions, but remember, you don't want your customer to feel like you're interviewing them for a podcast or taking a survey for a research study. You want to have a *conversation* with them. By asking these kinds of questions and digging deep, you are demonstrating that your sole and singular focus is to clearly identify what the customer's challenge is so that you can find out how best to help them. And, at the same time, you're digging down into the emotional reasons – the compelling reasons – why the customer is looking to buy, and importantly, what's going to drive them to buy from *you*.

So, how do we avoid it sounding like a formal interview script? We can use what are known as 'question softeners' to keep the conversation sounding natural. The best examples of question softeners are:

- *'Can I just ask…?'*
- *'By the way…'*
- *'Incidentally…'*

We also need to give the customer plenty of assurance that we are listening. By proving that we are listening to our customer, and I mean really listening, not only do we establish that all-important trust we've already discussed at length, but we can also confirm that we are understanding the customer correctly so that we can propose the best solution or product for them.

Eye contact and an occasional head nod are *not* enough to prove you are listening. My wife will tell you that I am an expert at the automatic eye contact, head nod and perfectly timed, '*Uh huh, I see, is that right?*' responses when, in fact, I haven't actually heard a single word! And, come on, let's be honest, we've all done it. Your customers have done it. They've probably done it *to you* when you were delivering some dull slide deck all about the history of your company (which, of course, you no longer do now that you're reading this book).

In reality, one of the best ways to demonstrate you are listening is to repeat back to the customer what they just said. You can repeat it verbatim (although not too often because that would sound fake), or better yet, you can paraphrase what they just said, followed by, '*Did I understand you correctly?*' or something to that effect.

And I always, *always*, take notes when the customer is talking so that I can repeat back, in summary, all the key issues that are most important to them. Each one gets its own bullet point in a dedicated section of my notes page. This allows you to prove you have been listening while taking on board their concerns, and it also provides you with an invaluable record of what problems you need to solve.

6

Identify the Decision-Maker: Who is the Gatekeeper?

Finding the People Who Can Say Yes

The great sales author and trainer Jeffrey Gitomer's sales strategy is very simple. He says, *'I put myself in front of people who can say yes, and I give value first.'* I have quoted Gitomer here exactly because I cannot improve upon this strategy.

But let's just spend a few moments focusing on the first half of this statement: putting yourself in front of people who can say yes. Whenever I'm coaching or training salespeople, I always ask what the most common objections are when trying to make a sale. Invariably, near the top of the list is, *'I need to go and speak with X'*. That *X* may be a spouse, a business partner, their boss or a purchasing manager. Sometimes the person your customer needs to speak with is not a fellow decision-maker themselves but an influencer or advisor, such as a friend, coach, consultant, colleague, subordinate or accountant. These are people who can't necessarily say yes, but they can definitely say no! If your customer doesn't have the ability to say yes, then the sales process has stalled and your ultimate goal of winning the sale is at risk, regardless of the strength of your product or your sales skills.

I was coaching the sales team of a long-established and reputable kitchen company, some of whom had been selling kitchens for the brand for the past 30 years. One salesperson shared his biggest frustration, which was then quickly seconded by his colleagues. It can take quite a while to sell a kitchen. After a prospective customer has taken a walk around the showroom, chatted with a salesperson, had a cup of complimentary coffee and then sat down to go into further detail about what they are looking for, the time spent could be upwards of three or four hours.

'And….?' I asked, *'What would happen then?'*

'Well,' the frustrated, 30-year veteran salesperson would go on to explain, *'we would go through all the details; the colours, the tiles, the set-up, the dates that they would want installation and so on. Sometimes the customer even had their measurements handy, which we just loved! It made our lives so much easier and showed real interest. But then I'd ask the customer for a deposit, and he or she would say, "I need to speak with my spouse."'*

'Ouch! That's gotta hurt! How long has this been going on?' I

would enquire, knowing full well what the answer was going to be. You guessed it: 30 years!

What was needed in this situation was customer qualification, and that has to be implemented at the very start of an interaction to make sure they are able to go the distance with you. And so, I spent the next 15 minutes or so talking them through my process to ensure this would never happen again. By the end of my talk – and I am not making this up – the 30-year veteran had his head in his hands. '*I cannot believe how simple that is.*' He said, '*How could I have overlooked this for so many years? All that time wasted with customers who couldn't even make a decision?*'

We call this experience a BFO, or a blinding flash of the obvious. Most of the really good ideas that make a difference in our lives turn out to be obvious. It's often just about taking the time to reflect and recognise what's going on.

'*It'll never happen again, I assure you,*' I reassured him. Or at least, it'll almost never happen again. '*Here's the strategy…*'

The Customer Qualification Process

So, what is the customer qualification process? There are essentially three important aspects we need to ascertain.

- We need to know whether they can say yes. In other words, are they the decision maker and what does their decision process look like?

- We need to know what their budget is.
- We need to know how serious they are about buying (and what their specific need or driver is).

Here we'll look at the first point in the qualification process, but budget will be covered next in the checklist, and we've already covered needs analysis above.

So, how do we identify whether they can say yes and, more specifically, who it is that makes the buying decisions? It's simple really: we need to ask. And, depending on your particular sales process and the specific situation, you probably want to ask very early on in the sales cycle to save yourself time. In the case of the kitchen company, we discussed the best approach for qualification in their context. They decided that the time to ask about decision-makers was after the customer had had a chance to wander around the showroom, drink a cup of coffee and build up some rapport through casual conversation, but before they sat down with the salesperson to go through the detailed requirements. In this way, they were not putting people off by turning them away too early and before they had had a chance to do some research, but they were saving their salespeople time and focusing in on the prospects that could produce a sale.

Let's first look at the questions we *shouldn't* ask when identifying decision makers. We can't ask, '*Are you the decision-*

maker?' This question can be insulting to the customer. You're basically saying, *'I need to decide whether you're worth spending time on. I need to find out who the real boss is so I can sell to them and not you.'* For the same reasons, we can't ask, *'Are you going to need to ask somebody else before you make a decision?'* So, what *do* we ask that won't offend or put people off?

Here's the qualification question I have found to be most effective (and diplomatic) in most sales situations:

'Who, other than yourself, will be involved in making this decision?'

It is incredibly important to respect the customer who is right in front of you, because even if that person can't say yes on their own, they can definitely say no. Plus, they are likely to be one of the key decision-makers, if not the only decision-maker. This is why we use the words '*other than yourself*.' Be sure to include and respect the customer in front of you at all times.

We use the words '*will be involved*' because we always want to assume, in the language we use, that the sale will go forward. We don't use words like '*would*' and '*might*' because they suggest we are doubtful that the customer will want to buy from us. We need to demonstrate one hundred percent confidence in our product or service and a belief that the customer will see the value and want to buy from us, and so our language needs to reflect that all throughout the sales process. By using the word '*involved*' we are also expanding the scope of the question to include not just the actual decision-makers but also any influencers. This includes anybody who will be giving the customer advice or counsel, particularly when it comes to larger purchasing decisions such as a new kitchen. I don't just want to know who the actual decision-makers are, I want to know about anybody who might chime in with advice and affect the sales decision.

Most importantly, this question often enables me to find out what the customer intends to do at the end of our conversation, and I want to know this at the very start. Let's look at an example answer to see how this works. When I ask the question, *'Who, other than yourself, will be involved in making this decision?'* a typical response from the customer might be, *'Well, if I like what you've got to show me, I'll need to go back and talk to my husband about it.'*

Great! That is all I need to know. By getting this information right at the start, I can determine how much time to spend with the customer, and I am also prepared for the objection that I now know I'm going to get at the end. In the case of the kitchen company, the salesperson might then respond as follows:

'Great, how about this for an idea? Why don't we invest a few minutes showing you around, we can answer any questions that you might have, and if you see anything you like, we can schedule a time for you to return to the store with your husband when we can talk in more detail. Does that sound okay?'

By the way, when you ask the above question just like

that, the customer always – *always* – says yes! And we like it when the customer says yes.

See what's happened here? We're not wasting time with a customer who cannot say yes on their own, but we are still initiating and building a relationship with them. We are respecting our customer and we are establishing *what happens next.*

And what happened with the kitchen company? It was a happy ending. They more than doubled their conversion rate, practically overnight, and reduced the amount of time they needed to spend with customers by nearly two hundred percent at the same time. What a result!

7

Find Out What Their Budget Is: Making it Affordable

If '*I need to go and speak with X*' is near the top of the most common objections heard by salespeople, then '*It's too expensive*' is at the *very* top, perhaps tied with '*I need to think about it.*'

We could spend a lot of time discussing pricing, but let's just deal with the question of budget here. If our aim as a salesperson is to be a problem solver, then our objective is to provide a solution to our customer's problem or need that *falls within their budget.* It's that simple. If the customer cannot afford the solution or if they are simply not willing to spend above a certain limit, then you will fail in your quest to solve their problem.

So, how do we address that issue early on? We have to ask an exploratory question or two to find out the customer's budget. *'Yes, but…,'* I can hear you beginning to ask. I hear, *'Yes, but…,'* a lot in my line of work as it happens. This particular one is usually followed by, *'My customers don't want to tell me their budget because they are afraid I'll use it to quote them the highest possible price.'* Either that or, *'They'll give me an extra low figure just in case I go high.'*

Well, I have a few thoughts on this issue that will hopefully help you in your sales process:

1. All you can do is ask. If the customer doesn't want to tell you then they won't, and you can't make them.
2. Where is the trust in your relationship? As a professional problem-solving salesperson, your first job is to get the customer to trust you, and in this situation, you are not trusting the customer to give you an honest answer about their budget. You will therefore invoke the 'law of attraction,' which, in essence, states that you get back what you put out in the world. Put out a lack of trust or a fear that your customer will not want to be honest with you about their budget, and that is exactly what will happen.
3. It's perfectly reasonable to ask about their budget, if you have established trust at the start by finding commonality and building rapport, and you have asked some good questions to establish what their needs are. In fact, it is *necessary* if you are going to solve their problem.

So, how to do it? Here's the question I usually ask:

'Obviously, finances are very important. Can I ask what budget you've set aside for this purchase?'

You can vary the language to suit your style or situation, but frankly, there is no need to change a single word of this question. Every element of it exists for a purpose.

In the first half, you are prehandling the financial objection by agreeing with the customer that finances – i.e. price – are an important consideration. Agreeing with a customer's objection, or even better, raising an objection *before* the customer does, relaxes them and encourages trust. They feel glad that you've raised the issue of price because it means they now don't have to raise it themselves. Nor do they need to worry that you are going to apply greater pressure to buy, which sadly is so often the case with bad salespeople.

In the second half, you are suggesting that the customer has already set aside a budget and has a number in mind (they often haven't). Even if the customer did not have a specific budget to start with, this prepares them to suggest a price range.

If, for some reason, the customer does not want to tell you a number, be it a range or a specific price, you may need to push a little bit further until you get some sort of guidance. After all, how can you possibly provide a solution that will meet the customer's needs if you don't know how much they are looking to spend? I might say something like this:

'I understand that perhaps you haven't given much thought to your budget, or had much of an idea about what this sort of item might cost, but if you could give me at least a ballpark range that I could work with, I can be sure to recommend the best possible solution.'

If appropriate and necessary, you could even go on to say:

'We've got different levels of product/service offerings, and I'm confident I'll be able to offer you a couple of options near the lower and higher ends of your budget.'

This assures the customer that they will have their need fulfilled without having to spend more than they wanted. It also subtly – or perhaps subconsciously – reminds the customer that there is no barrier to them going ahead with the sale.

If they *still* won't give you a budget (by the way, that's a warning light in my mind, and I would suggest you go back a couple of steps in the sales process to do further needs analysis or qualification, or perhaps ask a couple of temperature-checking questions – see below), I will put forward a range myself and then ask a temperature-checking question. For example, *'Based on what you've told me so far, Ms. Customer, we're probably looking at somewhere in the region of £2,000 to £3,000. How does that fit with what you had in mind?'*

When the customer is thinking about or answering that question, be sure to keep a look out for body language. That's often the bigger giveaway as to whether you are indeed in the right ballpark!

8

Know What (and When) Their Compelling Event Is: The Reason They Need You

What Is a 'Compelling Event'?

In most sales situations, whether it be B2B or B2C, commercial or domestic or wholesale or retail, customers tend to be in the market for a particular product or service because they have a need which is being driven by a specific event. That is, something which is happening or going to happen on a particular date, creating a need for the product or service.

A simple example in the domestic market would be a customer who is shopping for painting and decorating services because they are going to sell their house. Their compelling event is their house going on the market, and they know the date that will happen. They have to paint and decorate their house before that date so that it is appealing to prospective buyers.

I used to sell software testing services into large corporates, and the compelling events that we would look for in our sales situations were pretty straightforward: our client would set a target go-live date for the launch of a new system, and it needed to be tested, redeveloped and then retested all prior to that go-live date. The compelling event was the launch of the new system. However, a problem-solving salesperson could go even deeper than that. The launch of their new system wasn't the *real* compelling event. That would have something to do with *why* they are having to launch a new system in the first place. Perhaps they are releasing a new product, entering a new market or initiating a new marketing strategy. Maybe they just have certain customer service KPIs (key performance indicators) that they need to hit by a certain date in order to maintain some standard credential.

So, it's important to keep in mind that the 'why' a customer is in the market to buy your product or service may go much deeper than what's on the surface. And the problem-solving salesperson needs to understand this so that they can help the customer realise the importance of having the best solution for that problem… as well as the risk of not having the best solution!

Using the Compelling Event to Further Qualify Your Customer

Whatever the situation, by identifying our customer's compelling event and the relevant date, we have effectively deepened the qualification process; we now know that the customer has a genuine need and that there is an urgency as well. We can feel confident that the customer is not going to procrastinate, delay or "tyre-kick" ad infinitum: we can see where it sits in their priority list. What most salespeople hate – at least, the ones I speak with – is the customer that keeps saying, 'Yes, I do need to buy it. I will buy it. Just keep chasing me up because I'm busy with other things right now.' In other words, it's not a priority.

At the software testing company I worked for, in our sales teams, we were not allowed to include any prospect in our sales pipeline reports if we were not able to include details and dates around that customer's compelling event. If there was no compelling event - in other words, if there was no time-sensitive driver for the customer to buy - we could only classify them as a 'suspect' i.e. somebody that may have a need in the future but not imminently. If you wanted to break it down, you could say that there are three types of sales opportunities: those that have a compelling event, those where you have a 'hunch' they might buy and those where the customer assures you they are going to buy even though they can't give you a real reason why.

The compelling event principle made a radical and very effective difference to the way I conducted consultative selling over the years, but it may not necessarily apply to all types of businesses or customers. Nonetheless, there is almost always a compelling reason – if not an event with a date – for the customer to be in the market for your product or service; and, as problem solvers, we *must* know what that compelling reason is!

In summary, whenever possible, look for the compelling event and the corresponding date. Then, dig deeper and look for the 'real' compelling event that is driving it!

9

Offer a Compelling Guarantee: Removing Risk from the Equation

Why Is a Guarantee so Powerful for Customers?

When a customer is deciding whether or not to give you their money, particularly when it's the first time you're doing business together, what holds them back? Often, they are all wondering the same thing: *'Is this going to work?'*

There may be different variations of this question, but there is a common theme:

- *Is it going to do what the salesperson said it would do?*
- *Is it safe?*
- *Is it easy?*
- *Can I do it?*
- *Will I get my money's worth?*
- *Will I regret this?*

The severity of the customer's internal questioning will of course vary depending on the cost and consequences to them of the purchase, but the truth is, no matter how good your sales pitch is, the proof of the pudding will of course be in the eating. They won't know whether it will work until after they've paid for it, and therein lies the risk. The customer is worried that they are going to waste their money, or even worse, that they will lose face by making the wrong decision.

Let's consider an example. The software testing company I used to work for was small and not widely known. As part of our sales strategy, we commonly reminded ourselves of the old industry expression, '*Nobody got fired for using IBM.*' Our customers were often faced with a choice. To use us, a small, privately-owned company based in the North West of England that most people had never heard of, or to use a large, well-known brand such as IBM. IBM was, of course, more expensive than us, but they probably wouldn't do as good a job as us. However, if the final decision-maker chose IBM and the project went horribly wrong, nobody higher up the chain was going to shout, '*Why did you go with IBM?! What a risky decision!*' But if they chose us, and the project went horribly wrong, then the higher-ups would definitely shout, '*Who on earth is this mom-and-pop business in the middle of nowhere that you decided to risk such an important project on?!*'

Customers are always assessing the risk of using the

unknown as they want to experience the least possible risk. They desire security, reassurance, confidence and safety. They want calm. And it's our job as problem-solving salespeople to give it to them.

We might not be able to get around the fear of the unknown, but one of the best ways to give customers the reassurance they need is to offer a guarantee. A guarantee accomplishes two things. First, it gives the customer the certainty that they need in order to go ahead with you the first time. If it does all go wrong, they can extract themselves from the purchase without any penalties. If they know they have nothing to lose, it makes their decision a lot easier! Second, it expresses confidence in the quality of your product or service on your part. If you are actually willing to take the risk of failure on yourself – in other words, *'If the product doesn't work, it's my problem, Mr. Customer, not yours'* – then that must mean that you are pretty confident that it *will* work.

A guarantee is also a great way to differentiate yourself from the competition. If you guarantee your offering and the competition don't, then customers are not only more likely to go with you, but they may even be willing to pay a little bit more. After all, people will pay for quality and value. If you *do* offer a guarantee, it's important that you promote it clearly to customers and make it a core part of your offering. If your competition also offer a guarantee, but it's not very visible to customers, then this might still be enough to set you apart.

This is often the point in the conversation when the salesperson I'm coaching says to me, *'But I couldn't possibly offer to give all the customer's money back! What if they take me up on the guarantee and after manufacturing their product to spec and going through the hassle of delivering it, the customer then just demands their money back?'* Well, remember that, first of all, you don't have to offer a 100% money-back guarantee. You could offer a guarantee that you will fix any problems or address any issues within a specific timeframe. Or you might offer to replace any item with a similar item if the original isn't to the customer's liking. However, more importantly, the law dictates that whatever you sell cannot be faulty. If your product or service doesn't do what you said it would, you would be responsible whether you offered a guarantee or not. You therefore might as well turn the statutory law into a sales and marketing strategy that doesn't put you on the back foot – in fact one that engenders trust and differentiates you from the competition.

What Sort of Guarantee Should You Offer?

But what sort of guarantee should you offer? To work out what the best approach is for your business, you will need to test and measure. Try out different ideas and gauge which ones give you the best conversion rates. Where do you start though? Begin by putting yourself in your customers' shoes, or even better, by asking your customers a question:

- *What frustrates you the most when dealing with businesses in our industry?*
- *What worries you the most when making a decision to buy this product or service?*

You can even get more granular and look more closely at the different stages of the sales process:

- *What frustrates you most a) when trying to find our products or services, b) when going to buy our products or services, c) when going to pick up or receiving our products or services, d) when you're using our products or services, e) after you've bought our products or services…?* and so on.

Once you have the answers to these questions, you can offer a targeted guarantee that removes the most common worries or frustrations. In that way, you are focusing in on what the *customer* thinks is important rather than what *you* think is important. By being led by their worries, you are addressing the key stumbling blocks in the sales process.

Let's look at an example. My company, ActionCOACH, works with a plumbing company in the US. They identified the most common frustrations that customers have with plumbers. These were:

1. Plumbers arriving late or customers having to wait

in all day because no appointment time was specified.

2. Plumbers leaving a mess when they leave.
3. Plumbers not being able to fix the problem.
4. Plumbers having an unprofessional or unclean appearance.

The company put together a guarantee, which included specific answers to the above frustrations:

We guarantee that…

1. *You will be given an appointment window of no longer than one hour, and our plumbers will arrive within that window.*
2. *Our plumbers will leave the work area in your house as clean or cleaner than when they arrived.*
3. *Our plumbers will fix the problem on the first visit, or if they cannot, they will return at no extra charge to you until the problem is fixed.*
4. *Our plumbers will arrive in clean, branded vans and will be wearing clean, branded uniforms with name badges. They will remove their shoes before entering your home.*

Although it took a little time to pull together the right information in order to craft a targeted guarantee, it was worth the effort. By answering your customer's concerns before they even raise them, you will be clearing a path towards the sale.

10

Have Customer Testimonials at the Ready: Providing Social Proof

We all know that a customer can find out just about anything about you and your company with just a few clicks. More so than ever before, in this digitally connected world, your reputation precedes you. Reviews, testimonials, success stories, comments on social media; it never ends. It's easy for a customer to leave a bad review or comment online, which could remain there for the world to see *forever*! So, keeping your reputation intact is more important than ever before. But how do we do this?

Now, we won't dip into review sites such as Google Reviews and Trustpilot, but we do need to address the importance of customer testimonials. As a salesperson and as a professional problem solver, your job is (naturally) to recommend your company to your customers over the competition. Your customer knows this. So, while you are continuing to build trust with the customer, many will still need validation that they are not going to make a mistake going with you; and they need to get validation from elsewhere. The logical source for this reassurance is from other customers like them who have used you previously.

So, be sure to come to any sales situation armed with testimonials from past and current customers who are delighted with your service. I recommend having a mixture of written and video testimonials, as different customers have different communication preferences, which we've discussed in the first part of the book. It's important that they feel genuine, as customers can be suspicious of testimonials. They most definitely should not be anonymous or even vague. *'Excellent service! says Mrs. Smith, London'* does not fill me with a lot of confidence. In fact, it sounds entirely made up. Use full names and locations, possibly even specifying the product or service that was purchased, and ask your customers who provide testimonials for more specific details, such as *why* they feel it was excellent service. Show that you are proud of your testimonials in the way they are presented. Get a photo of your customers if they'll let you, and print your testimonials, case studies and success stories in full colour on high-quality, glossy paper. Talk with enthusiasm about that particular customer or the service you provided them when handing the testimonial to your prospect.

Video testimonials are even better. They are much harder to fake, so the customer will feel more reassured by this evidence. The customer giving the testimonial should still share their name and location to make it specific. Depending on the complexity of your product offering, your video doesn't need to be long. Some might be as short as thirty seconds or up to a few minutes long. You can get them done professionally – filmed, for example, by a videographer at the customer's place of business or their home if that's where the product was sold. Or you can get your smartphone out and wrap it up in a matter of seconds. Make sure that you keep getting new testimonials. You can't have too many! They must stay fresh as you want the customer to see recent experiences and they should reflect your latest product offering. Be sure to have a few questions handy when interviewing your customer for testimonials so that they know what information you're looking for. Otherwise, you might get non-specific comments such as '*Nice product.*' Some useful questions include:

- *Why did you choose us over other companies?*
- *What was the sales experience like?*
- *What was the after-sales experience like?*
- *Would you use us again in the future and why?*
- *What would you say to other people who are considering using our company?*

Make sure that you use your testimonials liberally. It's critical that you bring your testimonials with you to sales meetings. Here is a simple example to illustrate how you could introduce a testimonial into a conversation.

'Ms. Customer, you said your biggest concern was receiving regular communication from the supplier regarding their progress. Well, we have another customer, Mr. Y, who had the exact same concern, and here's what he said…'

Remember, you can also post them on your websites and social media and send them to prospects in the post or by email.

11

Ask Temperature-Checking Questions: Preparing for the Sale

Perhaps now would be a good time to explain the temperature-checking question. Commonly asked near the end of the sales process (and by commonly, of course, I mean *always*), the temperature-checking question's purpose is just that: to test how the customer is feeling about the solution you are presenting to them. However, the question can in fact be asked at just about any time during the sales process. Its purpose is to gauge whether you are leading the customer down the right path for them.

There are, of course, several variations to the temperature check, but here are my two favourites:

1. How does that fit with what you had in mind?

2. Which one fits best with what you had in mind? (when offering multiple options)

Not much explanation is needed here other than to say that this is one of the most valuable lessons you will likely take from this book. Essentially, when this question is asked prior to the 'close,' it vastly reduces your chances of getting a no from the customer. In theory, it should entirely eliminate your chances of getting a no.

The logic looks like this. If the customer's answer to the question, '*How does that fit with what you had in mind?*' is, '*Yes, this is what I had in mind,*' and you have done all your homework regarding qualifying them in terms of needs, budget and whether they are the decision-maker, then there should be no reason why they don't then go ahead with the sale. You've checked their temperature and they are good to go.

Almost as good an answer from the customer is: '*This does not fit with what I had in mind.*' In this instance, the customer is telling you important information which you can then use to guide them down a different path towards their solution. We then need to return to probing questions about their need, possibly starting with the question, '*Tell me more about that,*' or, '*Which part of the solution we've discussed so far does not meet with your expectations?*'

I have no intention of asking for the sale until I get an affirmative answer to the temperature checking question.

12

Ask for the Sale with Detail Questions: Getting the Customer Over the Line

In the sales industry, it is commonly believed that 70% of all lost sales occur because the salesperson did not *ask* for the sale. How crazy is that? It's the absolute foundation of the work we do, yet we shy away from it. Even if that statistic were only half correct, say 35%, it is still a depressing notion to consider that the salesperson went through all that work, from getting in front of the customer in the first place (or getting the customer into the store), to doing the qualification, the needs analysis, the presentations, and so forth, right through to offering the right solution to the customer, only to lose the sale because they did not actually ask the customer to buy. The customer loses out too because, without the right encouragement to move forwards with the sale, they'll probably offer an objection such as, '*Let me think about it*,' and then go away and get a cheaper, inferior product or service elsewhere. This is a lose-lose situation, and it's the salesperson's fault. *Your* fault!

Whatever the psychological or sociological explanations for this phenomenon, it simply remains the truth that customers often, if not always, have to be told what to do. In marketing and advertising, you have to tell customers to click here, clip this coupon, quote this promo code, visit our showroom, refer a friend. In sales, you have to tell customers, essentially, to sign here and get your wallet out.

My theory as to why so many salespeople fail to ask for the sale is that they are afraid. This is the part of the selling process where rejection happens. This is where salespeople suddenly have doubts as to whether their product or service is worth the cost. They worry about whether they have qualified the customer sufficiently and understood their needs. Or, more simply, they agonize over whether they are about to ruin the relationship with their customer that they worked so hard to build by asking for money. So, when the time comes, the salesperson hesitates. They hope that the customer will just ask whether they can buy it or pull their wallet out without being asked. And, of course, sometimes they do, and that's great. But most of the time you need to be bold and take control. As a professional problem-solving salesperson, remember that your job is to ask for an exchange of money for goods, and a reasonable customer will understand that.

So, how do we ask for the sale? If we're getting down to the nitty gritty, how do we ask for money? In short, we don't. We *assume the sale* and we ask *detail questions*. 'Assuming the sale' means exactly that. As problem-solving salespeople, we need to speak and behave as if we expect the customer to say yes. After all, we have made a professional, concerted effort to understand the customer's needs and expectations exactly, we have used our skills to offer the ideal solution based on these needs and we already know that our customer is a) the decision-maker, b) can afford it, c) needs or wants it, and d) for a specific reason (e.g. a compelling event).

Most importantly, we have already asked the temperature-checking question and we've received an affirmative answer. We asked, '*How does that fit with what you had in mind?*' and they replied with something like, '*It fits.*' Of course they did, otherwise we would not have moved to the next stage. The customer has told us that we have presented a solution that meets their needs exactly, and we must therefore assume that they want to go ahead. In this way, we don't actually have to ask for the sale explicitly – we simply start asking the detail questions.

But what are 'detail questions'? Let's pretend for a moment that the customer has just said to us, '*We would now like to go ahead and purchase this item, so what happens now?*' How would you respond? In most circumstances, you will reply with a detail question, thereby engaging the customer in the practicalities of the purchasing process and continuing to move the sales process forward.

Here are some example detail questions. Of course, you will need to choose ones that make sense within your industry or business and for your product or service:

- *How would you normally pay for this sort of item?* (i.e. the method of payment)
- *Is it better for you to come back in on a Tuesday or a Friday for your fitting?*
- *I'd like to set an appointment to come out to your home to do the initial survey, and I can do Wednesday morning next week. Does that work for you?*

And here's my personal favourite:

- *Would it be okay if I outlined what we need to do to get that underway?*

The reason I prefer the fourth question is that the answer to that question is always yes. Why wouldn't they want you to explain how they can take possession of your product or service? They've told you they need it or want it. They've told you they can afford it and that they can make a decision. They've told you that the solution you presented fits with what they had in mind. This is why it's okay for us to assume the sale. It's not about pretending to assume the sale. We genuinely believe the customer will buy because that is the only logical outcome of the sales process.

Once you've asked the detail questions to prompt the start of the purchase process, you can then begin the practicalities as if the customer has just told you they want to buy (which, of course, they essentially just have).

- *Great! First thing we need to do is take payment – will that be credit card, cash or bank transfer….?*
- *Great! Let's get that appointment in the calendar!*
- *Great! Come right this way so we can pick out your colour!*

See how this works? By following this process, at no point do you need to 'close' the sale or, even worse, ask the customer outright if they would like to go ahead. There are no yes/no questions and no tactics or tricks. If you assume the sale and begin to arrange purchase, you will come out on top much more often than not.

13

Stand By Your Price: Valuing What You Sell

How do you decide how much to charge for your products or services? Do you look at what the competition are charging? Do you move the price up and down and test and measure which price nets you the most sales or the most profit? Do you discount your price in order to get the sale or to drive customers through your door?

Your price is really an expression of confidence. What I mean by that is that the higher you set your prices, the more you clearly and genuinely believe your product or service is the best in the market. The cheaper you are, the less confident you appear that the customer is going to want to buy from you or is going to see value for money. Since you don't think much of your own value, you lower the price.

You need to be confident enough to show value to your

customers. Then you can sell on this value and not on price. If you do this, they will want the product more than they want the money. The higher your price, the more value you have to show. The more value you show, the more you can charge. The converse is also true: the lower your price, the less value you offer. And that's the message you're sending out to your customers. We're cheap and we don't offer you very much value.

Let the price-sensitive, discount-shopping customers go to your cheaper competition. They deserve each other. That customer will get an inferior product and your competitor will make little or no profit. They won't even get that customer returning for repeat business because they'll be coming back to you apologising for having made such a terrible mistake in the first place!

Better yet, why not raise your prices right now by 5% or 10%? A price hike across the board. Go on, I'll wait...

How do you feel? Are you excited, or are you a bit nervous? Remember this: worries about price are almost always in the minds of the business owner or salesperson. Customers are not as price-sensitive as they would have you believe, particularly when we are talking about small increases such as 5% or 10%. The two benefits of raising your prices are hard to ignore. First, the extra money that you make from raising your prices is pure profit. It goes straight on to your bottom line! Second, you can afford to lose a few customers who might leave because of your price increase, as that revenue loss will be more than covered by the extra revenue you're bringing in from the majority of customers who didn't even notice.

As an added bonus, those customers you did lose to price will likely be lower profit customers anyway – what we call C and D grade customers (as opposed to our A grade raving fans and B grade bread-and-butter customers). C and D grade customers tend to be complainers and problem customers, the ones who take up most of your and your team's time. They are probably awkward to sell to, they return items or demand extra follow-up visits and they beat you up on price at every sale, despite knowing that they are probably going to buy from you anyway. Frankly, you could do with losing them. By raising your prices, they might just head off to the competition – finally! – and dampen your competitors' spirits from now on instead of yours. At the same time, you are showing your A and B grade customers that you believe fully in the value of your company and your products, that you and your team are working tirelessly to provide them with a consistent and ever-improving quality service and that your new pricing structure reflects that.

You may be thinking: *'That's all well and good Andy, but I've had enough of the pep talk! Can you just advise me as to how best to come up with actual prices for my products?'* Oh alright, everybody likes a straightforward rule of thumb every once in a while. Here's my rule: you should get pushback on price about

20% of the time. What this means is that about one-in-five customers should either complain about your prices or mention that you are expensive, say no to the product based on price or negotiate hard with you because you are more expensive than the competition. If you're getting less than 20% pushback then you may be pricing yourself too cheaply. If you get no complaints or pushback at all, then you are *far* too cheap and need to make a change quickly! If more than 20% of your customers push back on price, then there is a possibility that you are a bit too expensive and may be pricing yourself out of some opportunities. On the other hand, being more expensive than most of the competition might be exactly where you want to be in the marketplace. If you prefer to work only with a certain class of customer, and your pricing model allows you to remain profitable and see sustainable growth, then by all means keep your pricing where it's at. However, that 20% pushback is a good benchmark if you're unsure of how to set your pricing.

Start recording and tracking your customers' responses to pricing now. Sure, it will take time to accumulate a useful sample of data, but it's worth it! In the meantime, if you take a moment to reflect, you will instinctively know roughly where you stand. Just look back at your last 10 sales situations and analyse your customer responses in each. Start with an educated guess for now, and then begin tracking for the future.

14

Offer Multiple Options at Different Price Points: Replacing Yes or No with 'Which?'

Why Is Having Multiple Options So Useful in a Sales Situation?

You will have probably heard that the most useful questions to ask are open questions. In other words, questions that cannot be answered with a yes or no. Open questions are best because they encourage people to open up with more detail and explanation – they move a conversation forward. This principle rings true in sales situations in most instances as well. For example, we want to avoid putting the customer in a yes or no situation when thinking about the sale. We don't want them asking themselves, '*Should I buy it, or shouldn't I?*' So the salesperson should never be asking, '*So, would you like to go ahead?*' This can stop the conversation dead in its tracks.

Much better is to ask them, '*Which of these options suits you best, Ms Customer: A, B or C?*' This gets the customer asking themselves, *Which one should I go for?* which moves the purchasing conversation forward and takes the no option off the table. Remember the multiple option temperature-checking question from an earlier chapter? That's where we want to get to!

Setting Options at Different Price Points

I prefer to offer three options, but at a minimum, there should be two options for the customer to choose from, and they should be at different price tiers. With three options, assuming of course that you know the customer's budget, have one option at or near the very top of their budget range, or even a little bit higher than their budget; have one option at the very low end of their budget; and then have one option right in the middle. All three options should still suitably meet the needs of the customer. When you present the different options, you will need to clearly explain the difference between them, why they are priced differently and how all three of them meet their needs in slightly different ways.

(A word of caution: avoid offering more than three options as this could confuse the customer and make it harder for them to make a choice. We want to make the customer's decision as simple and as easy as possible.)

It is generally agreed that, in most industries, about 70%

of customers will go for the middle option. Why? Well, first of all, often people don't want to be seen going for the cheapest option in front of their partner or companion, or surprisingly, even in front of the salesperson! Second, if the medium and higher-priced options are still within their budget, albeit more expensive, and they meet their needs, the customer can logically justify saying no to the cheapest option.

Many people will avoid the higher-priced option because they will feel that either of the lower-priced options suitably meet their needs, so why pay more than they need to? Therefore, logically, the middle option makes the most sense.

Having said that, you may be surprised at how many people still opt for the higher-priced option. If you have done a great job as a problem solver by ticking all the previous boxes in the sales process, and have clearly explained the difference between the three options and how the higher-priced option adds even greater value, many customers will be excited by the rewards of this choice and just go for it. Besides, remember that some customers, having been trained by bad salespeople over the years not to disclose their true budget, probably have more money to spend than they had let on previously.

At any rate, it is sensible to set your target price as the middle option and consider any customers that choose the higher-priced option as a bonus. Any customers that choose the lower-priced option still get a solution that meets their needs, and you still get a sale and a new, loyal repeat customer rather than a no.

15

Get Ready to Handle Objections: Being a Professional Problem Solver

Overcoming Objections

Handling or overcoming customer objections is generally the most common challenge raised by salespeople. This is the one they stress about the most; the one they ponder hopelessly about. This is interesting, when you consider that in almost all sales situations, even the ones that end with a positive result, the customer will raise at least one objection. Surely, given our experiences, we should be expecting objections. And, if we're expecting them, why aren't we prepared for it?

More than that, there is likely only a handful of objections that we will ever receive as salespeople. Certainly, there are no more than seven or so, and more likely only three or four. Obviously, this all depends on what type of business you are in and the products or services that you sell. If we know what sort of objections we are likely to encounter, why do we find it so difficult to know how to react to them? Let's look at the most common objections that salespeople I've trained tell me they get:

- *It's too expensive; it's beyond my budget.*
- *Let me think about it; I'll come back to you.*
- *I need to speak to my boss/spouse/partner.*
- *I'm not making a decision now; I want to shop around.*

This is all great news for you! If there are only a few objections that you are likely to get, then you can develop and perfect a system to handle and overcome objections most of the time. Even better, you can learn to 'pre-handle' the objections by raising them with the customer yourself, earlier in the sales process, so there is no objection in the customer's mind in the first place.

Why Are You Getting Objections?

Let's look at that strategy first. Why are you getting objections in the first place? Well, one reason is obvious, particularly when it comes to purchases that are more expensive: emotionally, the customer wants to buy and is excited about the purchase, but their logical, risk-assessing brain is running through what could go wrong.

What if it doesn't work? What if I like it now, but when I get it home, I decide I don't like it? What if I find the same item cheaper elsewhere? What if my spouse/partner doesn't like it? What if the after-sales service promised to me by the salesperson turns out to be poor or non-existent?

These are all legitimate objections to moving forward with the sale that the customer will be considering and, possibly, putting to you. They need to be satisfied that going ahead with this purchase is a good idea, and sometimes they need your help – the problem-solving salesperson – to alleviate their fears.

Another reason you get objections is because you caused them yourself because of information you gave (or didn't give) earlier in the sales process. Salespeople often suffer from TMI syndrome: giving too much information. The more facts and figures you sling at your customer, the more opportunity they have to come up with an objection to any of those facts, and they only need one objection to block the sale! Using a basic example, if you tell the customer: *'Our product folds up easily, making it easy to transport,'* your customer may think, *'That's not important; I'm not going to transport it.'* This alone may not block the sale, but each time you volunteer another piece of information that the customer doesn't care about, they may add that to a growing list of reasons not to buy. Or worse, the information will simply detract focus from what is actually important to the customer.

Focus the conversation on what the customer's problem or need is and how your solution is going to address their problem or need directly. Any bonus information on top of that is just going to raise your chances of getting an objection. Refer back to the questioning process: it's all about needs analysis. Did you ask the customer earlier on, '*Is transporting the product important to you?*' If the customer said no, then there is no need later on to mention that it folds easily. If the customer said yes, then it would certainly be beneficial to remind the customer that this is important to them and how the folding feature satisfies this need. Simply say, '*Mr. Customer, I remember you saying that transporting the product is important to you. Our product folds up easily, making it very easy to transport.*'

Before you tell the customer anything about your product, service or company, ask yourself, *Does the customer care about this feature? How is this relevant to their needs?*

Likewise, offering too little information can also raise an objection. If you don't communicate a piece of information to the customer that is important to them, such as whether there is a guarantee, they will raise it on their own and then object. You'll know what those missing pieces of information are because they will appear regularly in the common objections that you are getting from customers now. So, instead, let's *pre-handle* the objection. In other words, you should raise it before the customer does so that you can control the conversation and overcome the objection before it becomes a problem nearer the end of the sales process.

It will be disarming and it will help you to gain their trust.

As a simplistic example, if you frequently get the objection that your product is quite expensive, you might say something like this earlier in the process when you are still going through solutions and options: '*Mr Customer, I know you're probably thinking that this is quite expensive. In fact, most of my regular customers thought and said the exact same thing when they first bought from me. However,…*' You can use your own words, but you get the idea. Whatever objections you're getting now, raise them before the customer does.

So, to recap, once you have recognised where the objections are coming from you can reduce the number by either providing less information and focusing only on what is important to the customer, or by providing more information which addresses the most common objections directly and proactively so you can alleviate their fears.

How to Handle Objections

But, of course, we are still going to get objections no matter how proactive we are at preventing them. We need to be able to handle those objections effectively. The truth is, there is no excuse for not being excellent at this. You know you are going to get them and you know what they are going to be. So, to be blunt, you better figure out how you are going to address each and every objection you've been getting and what you are going to say. You should then script it out and practise, practise, practise. Once you're fully prepared, you will be so confident and professional that you'll be *glad* that they've raised the objection because you can handle it like a pro! Sound good?

Let's now take a look at how to handle the inevitable objections when they do come. The first thing to do when a customer raises an objection – no matter what it is – is to agree with them! Smile and say something like, '*You're right. I agree. I hear that a lot from my other customers.*' and so on. Right away this will set you apart from the typical salespeople your customer is used to dealing with; it will immediately reinforce the fact you are a trustworthy, professional problem solver. How come? Because your customer was expecting a different response from you, weren't they? They were expecting you to increase the pressure, sell harder, argue with them, *convince* them and even overrule or dismiss their objection. But all of these responses push them away. They make the atmosphere in the room uncomfortable, raising the temperature just a little bit more and making things awkward for the customer. In response, their emotions may suddenly shift direction. They may now feel like you just wanted the sale, regardless of their needs, or that they have disappointed or even angered you. It's a chain reaction and, ultimately, they end up feeling like they just want to leave.

Agreeing with the customer right off the bat serves one main purpose: to set them at ease. Let them know it's okay to have concerns, questions or issues they want to discuss. That's why you're here: to answer their questions and make them feel comfortable with whatever solution they choose; to give them all the information they need to make the best decision.

Once you've agreed with them and set their mind at ease, you then need to find out if there are any *other* objections. This is a very important part of the objection handling process and must not be skipped, so please pay attention. You then ask, *'Are there any other reasons besides <the objection just made> that would keep you from going ahead?'* Again, use your own language, but I would not change this one much. The key objective here is to get the customer to list any and all stumbling blocks to the sale.

When I was selling complex software testing projects into large companies such as banks and utilities, the sales process could take three to six months and the list of objections could be 20 or 50 objections long! Over a series of meetings or phone calls, I might have to ask this question dozens of times in different ways:

- *Is there any other reason why you would not want to go ahead?*
- *Are there any other concerns you have?*
- *Are there any other issues that might prevent us from moving forward?*

If there are multiple decision-makers, you may want to run the objections past all of them, proactively, to see what they need from you in order to move forward. For example:

- *Joe, Mary told me that she has concerns about <objection that was raised>, and I was wondering how you felt about that.*

Whether you are in a simple or a complex sales situation, you want to get *all* the objections out of *all* decision-makers first, before then working towards overcoming them.

When you've asked the, '*Are there any other reasons…*' question, if the customer says yes and offers you another objection, then do the same again. Listen intently, agree with the customer to keep them at ease, and then ask it again.

- *Great, thanks Mr. Customer. Are there any other reasons besides <objection 1> and <objection 2> that would keep you from going ahead?*

Be persistent. Keep following that questioning loop until the customer eventually says, '*Nope, those are the only reasons I've got for not going ahead.*' Once you've reached that stage and you believe you have exhausted all the objections, you can then move on and say:

- *Great! So, if <all listed objections> were no longer an issue for you, would you then be okay to go ahead?*

This is what is known as a conditional question. I am not yet answering their objection or even stating that I can. I only want the customer to agree that, on the condition I am able to answer the objection to their satisfaction, they will then go ahead with the purchase. If you want to call it a 'mini-close,' then feel free. The main thing to understand is that I am getting an agreement up front with the customer, so that if and when I do overcome their objections, they have already committed to moving forward. Remember the 'What happens next?' principle? We always want to have agreement with the customer up front so that, provided they are satisfied with the response, they will move on to the next step, in this case going ahead with the sale.

Imagine the opposite scenario occurring if we did not get the commitment up front: the customer tells me their objection, I answer the objection satisfactorily, and then the customer says, '*Great, thanks for that. Let me now go away and think about it.*' Salespeople grump to me about that all the time, but it's not the customer being ignorant. It's the salesperson not digging sufficiently for the real objection, or the hidden objection, and failing to get a commitment from the customer to move forward.

Back to the process. You've asked the customer if they would be okay to go ahead, assuming the objections they've just listed were no longer an issue for them. They must now answer yes or no.

If the customer says yes, then you have essentially closed the sale at this stage. The customer has agreed to buy from you, assuming you can answer their objections satisfactorily.

So, you now respond with, *'Great. Then let's invest some time looking at <each of these objections>.'* You must then work through each one with the customer until they are comfortable with the outcome and say something like, *'That makes sense. I'm okay with that,'* in response. Or, if you've had to make a change to your proposed solution in order to answer the customer's objection, you can go back to the temperature-checking question and ask again,

- *Now how does that fit with what you had in mind?*

Once you've arrived back at a solution that the customer is happy with, you can proceed again with the sales process as normal.

However, what if the customer says no to your question as to whether they'd be willing to go ahead, assuming that their objections were no longer an issue? In this case, there must be some other reason that's bothering them or causing hesitance. So, ask them:

- *There must be another reason you're concerned, then; do you mind my asking what that is?*

Once again, feel free to use your own words, as long as you are being honest and genuine with the customer and have their best interests as your number one goal. Once you've got that hidden objection out, you can then address it and reconfirm with the customer that you've answered all their concerns. We can then re-join the sales process by asking a detail question again.

Handling objections professionally is such an important skill. Just remember that it's okay to get objections. It's a natural part of the sales process, and the customer is not wrong for having them. They simply want to know that they are making the best decision. By raising an objection they are appealing to you, their professional problem solver, to help them through it. Rather than responding with panic and going into your shell or arguing with the customer, this is your opportunity to shine. You just need to hold your nerve and draw on your carefully prepared script to handhold them through the process. You know you are going to get objections, so there is no excuse for not being prepared. Make sure your sales process addresses the most common objections that you've had in the past, and make sure you are well-rehearsed for when you get those objections again. Above all, do not let all the hard work you've put in to building trust and rapport with the customer go to waste by applying additional sales pressure or by responding emotionally (other than sympathetically) to the customer's objection. Remember: whether or not the customer buys from you today, they will remember how you made them feel, and they will tell other people, good or bad.

16

Prepare for the Upsell: What's Your Extra?

Do You Want Fries with That?

Perhaps the most important question ever asked in business is: '*Do you want fries with that?*' asked by every pimply-faced teenager whoever stood behind a McDonald's fast-food chain counter. This question is what is known as an add-on sale or an upsell (depending on how you want to look at it). Back in the day, no matter what kind of burger or sandwich you ordered at a McDonald's, the employee who was taking your order would always respond with this question. And even though the upsell strategy was nothing new – car salesmen would offer you the extra shiny paint and the cruise control; every kitchen appliance or white goods company would offer you the extended warranty; leather goods shops would offer a leather care kit – McDonald's was the first to offer the *automatic* or systemised upsell on a grand scale. McDonald's employees were trained to ask this magic question of every single customer, no matter what. If they were caught not asking it, they were in trouble! Here's the amazing thing: one-in-three customers said yes to the upsell question. No selling was necessary. The McDonald's employee didn't try to convince you that their fries were great. They didn't offer you one to try. They didn't ask, *'Are you sure?'* if you said no. They just asked the question. And most customers didn't hesitate. It was an easy yes or no. The whole thing just happened automatically. But with that 33% conversion rate on the upsell, millions of dollars were added on to McDonald's bottom line worldwide just by asking the question. No selling necessary.

These days, *'Do you want fries with that?'* has been replaced with, *'Do you want to go large?'* because McDonald's now package their sandwiches and burgers into 'value meals' with fries and a drink. So, they've turned what used to be their upsell into their standard and offered a new upsell. And, if you're like me, you probably ask for the large before they get a chance to offer it, in which case the employee has been trained to automatically offer you some other side or dessert, such as onion rings, mozzarella sticks or an ice cream sundae.

The genius in this strategy is its simplicity: just ask. How often are McDonald's employees taught they need to ask the upsell question? Every. Single. Time.

Finding Your Upsell Opportunity

So…what's your fries? What do you need to start offering to your customers at every sale? What you want to look for here is something that is going to add value to the sale by adding value for your customer. This is very important, so allow me to repeat it. Be sure that your upsell *adds value for the customer*. My definition of 'pushy sales' is trying to sell the customer something they don't want or need. An upsell is something they might want or need and that will enhance their experience and enjoyment of the product. But if they don't want it, they don't want it, and that ends the conversation. Once you've got the main sale, there is no reason to push harder for the upsell. That McDonald's employee didn't care whether you took the fries; they were just told to ask the question.

Some companies I do sales training with raise concerns about the upsell strategy. They think they'll come across as pushy, aggressive or greedy, or that they may actually risk the main sale going ahead. To that I always respond: keep the faith. Remember that you have done everything else well. You've begun or built a relationship with the customer and they trust you. In fact, they trust you enough to have agreed to buy from you. It's okay to offer an upsell if it's of benefit to the customer or will add value to the existing sale. Keep in mind that most customers won't know about all the different products or services that you have to offer, and so you have a responsibility to educate them on all of the different options (or, at least all the different options that would be relevant or appropriate to that customer).

I remember when I had to start wearing prescription glasses. I returned to my local opticians after having my eyes tested to collect my new glasses: a nice pair of designer specs along with some prescription sunglasses. Later that evening, I went to clean my glasses, which were already building up a layer of grease and dust. I later learned that's quite common with high-value lenses. I was unable to clean the lenses adequately using tissue or a wet cloth, and I returned to the opticians the next day (my third visit by this stage) to ask for advice. They told me, *'You'll need to use this lens cleaner here. It costs £1.50.'* Of course, I said, yes please, and I went on my way. I was feeling happy that I now had the solution (literally) to my problem but annoyed that I had to make yet another trip to the opticians to get it, particularly as they could have offered me the cleaning solution at the same time that I collected my glasses. Not to mention, they knew this was my first pair of specs ever and that it was unlikely I was even aware of what was required to clean and maintain my expensive new purchases.

As a business coach, I was curious about their sales process and got to talking to the receptionist. She said they would have preferred to give the cleaning solution away for free because they hated asking for £1.50 when the customer had just paid them hundreds of pounds for new glasses. She said, *'We're not salespeople, and we don't want to be salespeople. We're here to help people, not take their money.'*

I understand how they feel. I work with a lot of medical and clinical businesses such as dentists, opticians and chiropractors, and they all tell me that they got into this business so they can help people, not sell products to them. But, as you are by now hopefully coming to realise if you haven't already, the only way we can help people is to sell to them. The only way we can help people is by taking their money. And they will be glad to give it if only we can help them. If my opticians sold me a cleaning solution, explained how to use it and told me the value of getting one, I would have been delighted. Instead, I was inconvenienced and annoyed because the optician was – well, let's be honest – scared to sell me a £1.50 bottle of cleaning solution. Crazy, isn't it? Especially considering they had just sold me about £400 worth of eyewear!

If I were coaching this optician, I would advise them to add something simple and direct to their script, such as: *'Here are your new glasses. Enjoy them – they look great on you! You'll need cleaning solution; it's £1.50. Shall I pop a bottle into the bag?'*

17

Be Ready to Negotiate: Finding that Win-Win

Getting Comfortable with Negotiation

Some salespeople find negotiating with a customer a frightening prospect. They become defensive and fall into attack mode in order to protect their bottom line, or they feel any back and forth over price will put their carefully built relationship under strain. But negotiating deals can be a natural and even enjoyable part of the sales process. Customers often expect there to be some negotiation, and professional negotiating can even strengthen the relationship between salesperson and customer when it's done correctly. Contrary to popular belief, it's not about compromising, which often ends in a lose-lose situation as both parties give up more than they want just to find a solution. In contrast, the purpose of any sales situation, and of negotiation, is a win-win: the customer gets the best solution for them, and the salesperson gets a sale. There is no better way to open a negotiating conversation by reminding the customer of this and agreeing on an objective:

'The purpose of this meeting is to find out exactly what you want and what you need, and to share with you exactly what I'm going to need, so that we can work together and arrive at the ideal solution for both of us.'

The world of negotiation is vast, and there is not enough room in this book to go into depth. At my company, ActionCOACH, we recommend books and training courses to help salespeople develop advanced negotiation skills, but it is worth covering a few top tips here that you can integrate, quickly and easily, into your sales meeting checklist.

Top Tips for Negotiation in Your Sales Meeting

The key to professional and successful negotiations is preparation, so top tip number one is to know exactly what you want to get out of it. As in any sales meeting, be clear on your objectives before you go in. The clearer you are on the objective, the more control you can retain of the meeting's direction, and that will help to guide you towards your goal.

Top tip number two, again belonging to the preparation phase, is to be absolutely clear on what you *don't* want. In other words, what is your minimum acceptance level? In negotiations, the general idea is that the other party is going to want you to give something up or give something extra, in exchange for them having to give something up or give something extra. That is absolutely fine, but you also need to know how far you are willing to go to get what you want before you eventually have to say no and walk away. And remember to stick to your guns. If you are not going to walk away from the negotiations happy with the deal, then there is no deal. In these situations, the best way to handle it is by being direct and honest: *'Unfortunately, I'm not going to be able to meet that condition, and here's why…'* You may then want to add, *'But it may be worth exploring other options…'*

Top tip number three occurs during the negotiation itself as opposed to during preparation. Make sure that for every single thing you give away or give up – a price discount, an add-on or an earlier delivery date – you get something in return. There is never a something-for-nothing in a negotiation. No matter how small it is, to maintain a position of strength and respect with the other party, you must ask for something that is of benefit to you.

Top tip number four is about making sure the customer comes away feeling satisfied. Negotiating isn't just about you getting what you want. You must also make sure that the other party is happy with their end of the deal. The great entrepreneur, James Caan of Dragon's Den, explained in his excellent book, *The Real Deal*, that whenever he gets ready to shake hands with the other party at the end of a negotiating session, he always asks them if they, too, are happy with the deal. He may even ask, '*Are you sure?*' several times because he wants to be certain they don't feel they gave away too much. This is so important because if your customer feels hard done by then it is going to damage the relationship between you in the long-term, which will make it harder to do business with them in the future. You may even experience the after-effects in the short-term, say in their attitude the next time you communicate with them. They may be thinking, '*I wonder how they are going to take advantage of me this time!*' Remember, the goal of negotiations is not to win. It's to find a win-win.

18

Be Persistent: Keep Following-Up

The Value of Persistence

Consider these statistics taken from ActionCOACH:

48% of salespeople never follow up with a prospect.

25% of salespeople follow up with a prospect once and then give up.

12% of salespeople follow up with a prospect twice and then give up.

Only 10% of salespeople follow up with a prospect three or more times.

And now the painful bit:

2% of sales are made on the first contact.

3% of sales are made on the second contact.

5% of sales are made on the third contact.

10% of sales are made on the fourth contact.

80% of sales are made on the fifth to 12th contact.

Now we all know that 78% of statistics are made up (that's a joke; remember, get your customer laughing), but even if these numbers aren't perfectly accurate in your industry, the principle is still relevant and possibly quite alarming for you. These numbers tell us that most salespeople are giving up long before they would have won the sale and that they would get many more sales if they just persisted with follow-ups.

A Process for Following-Up

But it's not enough to just decide you are going to be more persistent. Be sure to include in your sales process – your checklist – a *process* for following up. Decide how and when you are going to follow up with the prospects who said no, or, '*Not now*,' or, '*Let me think about it*.' How long will you leave it? Two days? Two weeks? Three months? Whatever the time period you choose, be sure to keep in touch with 'future' customers by continuing to add value to their lives and not just 'chasing' them. For example, send them an email offering a suggestion that will improve their business. Make them aware of an event you've got coming up, and send them a personal invitation. Send them a handwritten thank-you note for taking the time to talk to you about your product. Send them a video email saying how much you enjoyed meeting them.

Whatever methods you choose (and you'll need more than one method, to mix it up a little and keep it fresh), this will ensure you stay at the forefront of their mind so that, when they are ready to buy, they'll remember how you made them feel the last time you connected with them.

Get creative. Look up your customers on LinkedIn or even Facebook to find out what their interests are, and then send them something relating to that interest. Simply say, *'I found this article online and thought you might be interested.'*

Use your customer relationship management (CRM) system to track your activity. Take notes about the last interaction so you can remember the next time you connect with a customer. Track the methods you are using with each customer so you can mix it up, or do the opposite and continue using the communication methods that are best received by each particular customer. A CRM system will also help you make sure that you don't forget about customers, so even if they're not 'hot' now, they're not going to quietly fade away over time. Do whatever works best for you, but be sure to manage all your activity with a robust database system.

Finally, don't assume the worst: be positive about what can change in the future. Remember that just because a customer says no to you, it doesn't mean that they went and bought somewhere else. They may have gone away and thought about it and decided that now was not the right time to purchase that product. When you reconnect, a few weeks or a few months down the road, it might turn out to be a better time for them, and they may just need that friendly nudge from you in the right direction.

Summary: Putting it into Practice

So, there you have it. You now have the foundations needed to implement this learning effectively and to become a great salesperson – an expert problem solver with empathetic communication skills. This is excellent groundwork to be able to execute your sales checklist. Let's take a step back and make sure we're happy with the list we've built:

- ✓ Have a Script: Practise, Practise, Practise
- ✓ Build Rapport: Establishing Your Relationship
- ✓ Use a Statement of Intent: Getting Your Customer on Board
- ✓ Have an Objective: What Happens Next?
- ✓ Understand Their Needs: It's All About the Questions
- ✓ Identify the Decision-Maker: Who Is the Gatekeeper?

- ✓ Find Out What Their Budget Is: Making it Affordable
- ✓ Know What (and When) Their Compelling Event Is: The Reason They Need You
- ✓ Offer a Compelling Guarantee: Removing Risk from the Equation
- ✓ Have Customer Testimonials at the Ready: Providing Social Proof
- ✓ Ask Temperature-Checking Questions: Preparing for the Sale
- ✓ Ask for the Sale with Detail Questions: Getting the Customer Over the Line
- ✓ Stand By Your Price: Valuing What you Sell
- ✓ Offer Multiple Options at Different Price Points: Replacing Yes or No with 'Which?'
- ✓ Get Ready to Handle Objections: Being a Professional Problem Solver
- ✓ Prepare for the Upsell: What's Your Extra?
- ✓ Be Ready to Negotiate: Finding That Win-Win
- ✓ Be Persistent: Keep Following Up

These are the 18 fundamentals any professional salesperson must have in place to be consistently successful in sales. Keep in mind that not all 18 may be required in any given situation. For instance, you may not need to handle objections with one customer. Another customer may be ready to buy without having to see your customer testimonials. A compelling event may not always need to be present for a customer to buy.

What I can guarantee, however, is that if you are sitting in your car outside your prospect's home or office, and you can confidently put a checkmark next to each of these 18 items before you go in, *you will* have amazing sales success. And this is all I wish for you!

Now it's time to take action! Get started building your script using this list, keep testing and measuring as you implement, and never give up. There has never been a better time to invest in yourself, to commit to learning and to develop and fine tune your sales process. Good luck. I look forward to hearing about your success.

About the Author

As one of the top coaches in ActionCOACH in the UK and globally, Andy Goldberg brings over 25 years of remarkable leadership, sales, business and personal development experience to executives and business owners. An award-winning coach since 2010, he specialises in sales, leadership and improving team performance and culture.

Andy's brand promise to growth companies is simple: to help committed business owners to grow their business at a faster rate, achieve record results and get more life from their business.

To fulfil these promises, Andy defines what he does in four words:

- Awareness: He helps you see things that you cannot see in yourself and your organisation. These can be opportunities or challenges.

- Education: He brings proven strategies into your learning in leadership and management, sales and marketing, recruitment, strategic thinking and execution planning, communication adapting and business and personal development.
- Implementation: He assists you in thinking through and putting this education into practice through your daily activities.
- Discipline: He holds you accountable to your goals and the actions that you commit to.

As a business coach, Andy is an 'all-rounder' but particularly enjoys and specialises in sales, leadership and improving team performance and culture.

Andy graduated from the University of Michigan with a Bachelor of Arts degree in Chinese Studies, which he has found to be not even the least bit useful. He is also competent in French and Spanish. Coming to Scotland from the USA in 1998, Andy's most difficult linguistic challenge to date has been understanding Glaswegians.

Andy is certified and supported by the world's #1 business coaching team, ActionCOACH Business Coaching.

For more information, visit:

https://andrewgoldberg.actioncoach.co.uk

Acknowledgements

Although this is a short book, there are nonetheless many people who have helped me immeasurably over the years, some directly and some indirectly. I would first like to thank those who have inspired me to finally get my finger out and write the book in the first place.

Andy Hemming, my coach, who wrote an amazing book himself, *Think Smarter*, and advised me all the way through my book writing journey. James Malinchak, whose public speaking course, "Big Money Speaker," was truly educational and inspiring. Darren Hardy, whose "Darren Daily" videos I watch every morning and whose book, *The Compound Effect*, I have read and absorbed several times. And, finally, Brad Sugars, founder and chairman of ActionCOACH, who is the reason I chose to become an

ActionCOACH business coach myself 12 years ago.

I would also like to thank Monte Wyatt, who coached me through many of the early years in my coaching career and got me through the bad times to get to the good.

Thank you to Sarah Busby, who held my hand every step of the way during the creation of my first book, with structure, editing and language. Sarah's diligence, persistence and patience continued to remind me that writing a bad book might be easy, but writing a good book definitely isn't.

Thanks also to David Prendergast for the design, formatting and illustrations in the book.

Very special thanks must go to all of my coaching clients over the years who trusted me and were willing to invest in their own business education in order to grow themselves and their businesses. You are the reason I keep going every day.

And finally, I have never-ending gratitude for my loving wife and family for their constant support throughout my sales and coaching career. Sales isn't easy (if it was, everybody would be doing it), and to have so much love and support behind me through the ups and downs was absolutely critical.